A Book Of

PERFORMANCE MANAGEMENT

For

MBA (HRM) Semester - III
As Per Pune University's Revised Syllabus
Effective from June 2014

Mrs. Archana Vechalekar Sadolikar
B.Com, MBA (HR)
Assistant Professor
ZES's Dnyanganga Institute of Career Empowerment and Research
Narhe, Pune.

N2144

MBA - SEM. III : PERFORMANCE MANAGEMENT ISBN 978-93-5164-049-3

First Edition : **July 2014**

© : **Author**

The text of this publication, or any part thereof, should not be reproduced or transmitted in any form or stored in any computer storage system or device for distribution including photocopy, recording, taping or information retrieval system or reproduced on any disc, tape, perforated media or other information storage device etc., without the written permission of Author with whom the rights are reserved. Breach of this condition is liable for legal action.

Every effort has been made to avoid errors or omissions in this publication. In spite of this, errors may have crept in. Any mistake, error or discrepancy so noted and shall be brought to our notice shall be taken care of in the next edition. It is notified that neither the publisher nor the author or seller shall be responsible for any damage or loss of action to any one, of any kind, in any manner, therefrom.

Published By :
NIRALI PRAKASHAN
Abhyudaya Pragati, 1312, Shivaji Nagar,
Off J.M. Road, PUNE – 411005
Tel - (020) 25512336/37/39, Fax - (020) 25511379
Email : niralipune@pragationline.com

Printed By :
Repro Knowledgecast Limited,
Thane

DISTRIBUTION CENTRES

PUNE

Nirali Prakashan
119, Budhwar Peth, Jogeshwari Mandir Lane
Pune 411002, Maharashtra
Tel : (020) 2445 2044, 66022708, Fax : (020) 2445 1538
Email : bookorder@pragationline.com

Nirali Prakashan
S. No. 28/27, Dhyari,
Near Pari Company, Pune 411041
Tel : (022) 24690371
Email : dhyari@pragationline.com
bookorder@pragationline.com

MUMBAI

Nirali Prakashan
385, S.V.P. Road, Rasdhara Co-op. Hsg. Society Ltd.,
Girgaum, Mumbai 400004, Maharashtra
Tel : (022) 2385 6339 / 2386 9976, Fax : (022) 2386 9976
Email : niralimumbai@pragationline.com

DISTRIBUTION BRANCHES

NAGPUR
Pratibha Book Distributors
Above Maratha Mandir, Shop No. 3, First Floor,
Rani Jhanshi Square, Sitabuldi, Nagpur 440012,
Maharashtra, Tel : (0712) 254 7129

BENGALURU
Pragati Book House
House No. 1, Sanjeevappa Lane, Avenue Road Cross,
Opp. Rice Church, Bengaluru – 560002.
Tel : (080) 64513344, 64513355,
Mob : 9880582331, 9845021552
Email:bharatsavla@yahoo.com

JALGAON
Nirali Prakashan
34, V. V. Golani Market, Navi Peth, Jalgaon 425001,
Maharashtra, Tel : (0257) 222 0395
Mob : 94234 91860

KOLHAPUR
Nirali Prakashan
New Mahadvar Road,
Kedar Plaza, 1st Floor Opp. IDBI Bank
Kolhapur 416 012, Maharashtra. Mob : 9855046155

CHENNAI
Pragati Books
9/1, Montieth Road, Behind Taas Mahal, Egmore,
Chennai 600008 Tamil Nadu, Tel : (044) 6518 3535,
Mob : 94440 01782 / 98450 21552 / 98805 82331, Email : bharatsavla@yahoo.com

RETAIL OUTLETS

PUNE

Pragati Book Centre
157, Budhwar Peth, Opp. Ratan Talkies,
Pune 411002, Maharashtra
Tel : (020) 2445 8887 / 6602 2707, Fax : (020) 2445 8887

Pragati Book Centre
Amber Chamber, 28/A, Budhwar Peth,
Appa Balwant Chowk, Pune : 411002, Maharashtra,
Tel : (020) 20240335 / 66281669
Email : pbcpune@pragationline.com

Pragati Book Centre
676/B, Budhwar Peth, Opp. Jogeshwari Mandir,
Pune 411002, Maharashtra
Tel : (020) 6601 7784 / 6602 0855

PBC Book Sellers & Stationers
152, Budhwar Peth, Pune 411002, Maharashtra
Tel : (020) 2445 2254 / 6609 2463

MUMBAI
Pragati Book Corner
Indira Niwas, 111 - A, Bhavani Shankar Road, Dadar (W), Mumbai 400028, Maharashtra
Tel : (022) 2422 3526 / 6662 5254, Email : pbcmumbai@pragationline.com

www.pragationline.com info@pragationline.com

Preface ...

The main focus of performance management is to enable employees understand the performance standards and what it takes to sustain performance for a longer period of time and also how to improve it further. It also involves developing individual employees' commitment towards the organisation by improving their levels of performance. This in turn helps in matching the required amount of competencies to be possessed by the employees.

This book is specially designed for the students of MBA Semester III, HRM specialisation where they get an idea of the important aspects of performance management. The idea here is to make the students aware of various concepts such as the performance management process, ethics in performance management, difference between performance appraisal and performance management, implementing performance management system in the organisation, matching organisational culture with the performance management system and many more.

Performance management is now gaining an important place in organisations. It not only helps the employees to boost their performance but also helps the organisation to retain talented employees. Performance management always promotes personal growth and growth in the career of employees by helping them understand their goals and the achievement of those goals by enhancing their knowledge and skills.

The book covers all the topics as per the syllabus prescribed by University of Pune. It is designed keeping in mind the needs of students and requirements of the industry. The book is divided into 5 chapters and covers all the concepts related to performance management including meaning, definition, importance, process, rewards in performance management etc.

I thank **Shri Dinesh Bhai Furia** and **Shri Jignesh Furia** of Nirali Prakashan for giving me an opportunity to write this book. I also would like to express my gratitude to the team of editors, proofreaders, artists and typists for their hard work and constant support in the process of publishing this book.

Last but not the least my sincere appreciation and gratitude to our esteemed readers.

Utmost care has been taken to ensure that there are no mistakes or errors in the text, however, any comments or suggestions for further improvement in the text of this book will be gratefully acknowledged and appreciated.

Mrs Archana Vechalekar Sadolikar

Syllabus ...

1. Introduction to Performance Management System

Definition, concerns and scope - Historical developments in Performance Management - Performance appraisal Vs. Performance management - Performance management Vs. Human resource management - Processes for managing performance - Essence and Implications of Performance Management-Critical appraisal

2. Performance Management Process

Performance planning, Setting objectives - Organisational and individual performance plans - Components of Manager's performance and development plan - setting mutual expectations and performance criteria.

Performance Managing, Objectives of performance managing, Process of performance managing, Importance of performance managing. Performance Appraisal, Objectives of performance appraisal. Process of performance appraisal, Types of performance appraisal, Achieving effective performance appraisal. Monitoring and Mentoring, Introduction - Supervision - Objectives and Principles of Monitoring - Monitoring process - Periodic reviews - Problem solving - Engendering trust - Role efficacy.

3. Implementing Performance Management

Strategies for effective implementation of performance management - Top management agreement commitment and leadership, Building performance oriented work culture. Factors affecting effective use of performance management - Corporate culture, alignment, Review and update.

4. Reward for Performance

Reward system, Components of Reward System, Objective of Reward System, Linkage of performance management to reward and compensation System performance management pitfalls and remedies, Recognising the problems and Pitfalls, Limitations, Shortcoming or efficiencies of performance appraisal, Guideline for performance appraisal and good practices.

5. Ethics in Performance Management

Ethical performance Management Defined, Objectives and Significance of Ethics in Performance Management, Ethical issues and dilemmas in Performance Management, Ethical Strategies in Performance Management, Performance Management in Multinational Corporations.

Contents ...

1. Introduction to Performance Management System — 1.1 – 1.22

2. Performance Management Process — 2.1 – 2.32

3. Implementing Performance Management — 3.1 – 3.22

4. Reward for Performance — 4.1 – 4.30

5. Ethics in Performance Management — 5.1 – 5.16

Case Studies — C.1 – C.15

Multiple Choice Questions — MCQ.1 – MCQ.14

Chapter 1...

Introduction to Performance Management System

Contents ...

1.1 Performance Management
    1.1.1 Introduction
    1.1.2 Definitions of Performance Management
    1.1.3 Characteristics of an Effective Performance Management System
    1.1.4 Objectives of Performance Management System
    1.1.5 Concerns of Performance Management
    1.1.6 Scope of Performance Management
    1.1.7 Historical Developments in Performance Management
    1.1.8 Advantages
    1.1.9 Disadvantages
1.2 Performance Appraisal Vs. Performance Management
1.3 Performance Management Vs. Human Resource Management
1.4 Process of Performance Management
1.5 Processes for Managing Performance
1.6 Essence of Performance Management
1.7 Implications of Performance Management
- Points to Remember
- Questions for Discussion
- Project Questions

Learning Objectives ...
- To understand the definitions, concern and scope alongwith the historical developments in Performance management
- To learn the difference between Performance appraisal and performance management
- To understand Performance Management Vs. Human Resource management

- To learn the process for managing performance
- To understand the essence and implications of Performance Management – critical appraisal

1.1 Performance Management

1.1.1 Introduction

Performance Management consists of activities which ensure that goals are consistently being met in an effective and efficient manner. Today, all the major activities of HR are driven towards development of high performance leaders and fostering employee motivation. So the role of HR in today's context has changed from being just an appraiser to a facilitator / enabler. The process of performance management begins when any new employee joins the organisation and ends when the individual quits from the organisation. We can also say that performance management is a systematic process by which the entire organisation's performance can be enhanced by improving the performance of the individual within a team framework.

1.1.2 Definitions of Performance Management

Managing employee performance and aligning their objectives, facilitates the effective delivery of goals. There is a clear and immediate correlation between using performance management programmes for improved business and organisational results, as employees are the most important contributors in the success or failure of any organisation. Performance Management can focus on the performance of an organisation, a department, an employee, or even the processes to build a product or service. Performance Management basically prepares the employees by improving their competencies to meet present and future challenges. It typically involves three phases:

- Planning,
- Monitoring and
- Rewards.

Good planning begins with analysing the exact goals the organisation needs to attain and to develop realistic ways to achieve them. Monitoring during performance management involves not just monitoring the progress of each department and employees but also providing them with constant feedback whether it is in the form of praise and reward or in constructive criticism. Rewards can improve morale, boost productivity and help move closer to goals. If performance management is to be successful, the rewards need to be utilised.

1. **Armstrong and Baron (1998)**

   "Performance Management is both a strategic and integrated approach to delivering successful results in the organisation by improving the performance and developing the capabilities of teams and individuals."

2. **Gary Dessler**

   "Performance Management is a process that consolidates goal setting, performance appraisal, and development into a single, common system, the aim of which is to ensure that the employee's performance is supporting the company's strategic aims."

   ➢ Performance Management is the continuous process of
   - Identifying
   - Measuring
   - Developing the performance of individuals and teams.
   - Aligning performance with strategic goals of the organisation.

   Performance management is *an ongoing process of communication between a supervisor and an employee that occurs throughout the year, in support of accomplishing the strategic objectives of the organisation.*

1.1.3 Characteristics of an Effective Performance Management System

(a) **Objectives should be Clear:** The objectives of the appraisal should be clear and specific. An effective performance system will always have specific appraisal attributes to match the employee's job description.

(b) **Data should be Valid and Reliable:** An effective performance appraisal system provides data that is consistent, reliable and valid. It supplies data according to the objective that serves the purpose of performance appraisal and succession planning.

(c) **Performance Criteria should be well Defined:** An effective performance appraisal has standard appraisal forms, rules and appraisal procedures. It will have well defined performance criteria and standards.

(d) **Economical and Less Time Consuming:** Effective performance appraisal systems are designed to be economical and less time consuming to bring maximum benefits.

(e) **Should Initiate Follow Up:** A post appraisal talk should be arranged for employees to get feedback from their managers. It also helps the organisation to learn about the problems and difficulties the employees might be facing and discover suitable training methods.

Performance appraisal is one thing that not done properly can harm the organisation and the employees by creating conflicts. An organisation that has conflicting teams at work can never prosper. Therefore, choosing an effective performance appraisal system is a wise thing to do.

1.1.4 Objectives of Performance Management System

A performance management system consists of the processes used to identify, encourage, measure, evaluate, improve, and reward employee performance at work. Employees' job performance is an important issue for all employers. However, satisfactory performance does not happen automatically; however, it is more likely with a good performance management system.

Appraisal serves a twofold purpose: (1) to improve employees work performance by helping them realise and use their full potential in carrying out their firm, missions and (2) to provide information to employees and managers for use in making work related decisions. More specifically, appraisals serve the following purposes:

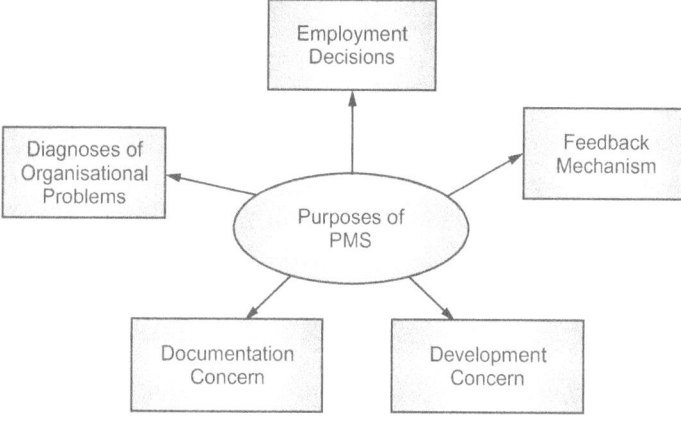

Fig. 1.1

(1) **Feedback Mechanism:** Appraisals provide feedback to employees therefore serving as vehicles for personal and career development. Performance appraisals must convey to employees how well they have performed on established goals. It's also desirable to have these goals and performance measures mutually set between the employees and the supervisor. Without proper two-way feedback about an employee's effort and its effect on performance, we run the risk of decreasing his or her motivation.

(2) Development Concern: Once the development needs of employees are identified, appraisals can help establish objectives for training programmes. It refers to those areas in which an employee has a deficiency or weakness, or an area simply could be better through effort to enhance performance. For example, suppose a college professor demonstrates extensive knowledge in his or her field and conveys this knowledge to students in an adequate way. Although this individual's performance may be satisfactory, his or her peers may indicate that some improvements could be made. In this case, then, development may include exposure to different teaching methods, such as bringing into the classroom more experimental exercises, real world applications, internet applications, case analysis, and so forth.

(3) Documentation Concern: A performance evaluation system would be remiss if it did not concern itself with the legal aspects of employee performance. The job related measure must be performance supported when an Human Resource Management (HRM) decision affects current employees. For instance, suppose a supervisor has decided to terminate an employee. Although the supervisor cites performance matters as the reason for the discharge, a review of this employee's recent performance appraisals indicates that performance was evaluated as satisfactory for the past two review periods. Accordingly, unless this employee's performance significantly decreased (and assuming that proper methods to correct the performance deficiency were performed), personnel records do not support the supervisor's decision. This critique by HRM is absolutely critical to ensure that employees are fairly treated and that the organisation is "protected". Additionally in cases like sexual harassment, there is a need for employees to keep copies of past performance appraisals. If retaliation such as termination or poor job assignments occurs for refusing a supervisor's advances, existing documentation can show that the personnel actions were inappropriate.

Because documentation issues are prevalent in today's organisations, HRM must ensure that the evaluation systems used support the legal needs of the organisation.

(4) Diagnoses of Organisational Problems: As a result of proper specifications of performance levels, appraisals can help diagnose organisational problems. They do so by identifying training needs and the knowledge, abilities, skills, and other characteristics to consider in hiring, and they also provide a basis for distinguishing between effective and ineffective performers. Appraisals therefore represent the beginning of a process, rather than an end product.

(5) Employment Decisions: Appraisals provide legal and formal organisational justification for employment decisions to promote outstanding performers; to weed out marginal or low performers; to train, transfer, or discipline others; to justify merit increases (or no increases); and as one basis for reducing the size of the workforce. In short, appraisals serve as a key input for administering a formal organisational reward and punishment system.

1.1.5 Concerns of Performance Management

The concerns of Performance Management are as under:

(1) **Concerned with the Output:** The output is nothing but the results achieved, outcomes, processes required for reaching the results and also inputs like knowledge, skills, and attitude required to meet the output.

(2) **Concerned with the Measurement of Results:** The result measurement must be done accurately and with a lot of care, since the rewards and/or punishments are solely dependent upon the measurement of output. This also involves review of progress in the achievement of set targets.

(3) **Concerned with Planning:** While any organisation is planning for performance management activity, it must have the business plan ready. Having a proper plan in place shapes the future activities in a positive way.

(4) **Concerned with Continuous Improvement:** Performance standards will not be achieved until and unless there are regular and continuous improvements in the current processes and practices. Continuous improvement leads to continuous development which in turn creates learning culture and an open system of communication.

(5) **Concerned with Establishing Appropriate Culture:** Establishing a culture of trust and mutual understanding that fosters free flow of communication at all levels in matters such as clarification of expectations and sharing of information on the core values of an organisation which binds the team together.

(6) **Concerned with the provision of procedural fairness and transparency** in the process of decision making.

1.1.6 Scope of Performance Management

(1) **Identifying Performance Parameters:** When any organisation decides to go for performance management activity, it is very important to decide the parameters of

performance, because when the parameters are clear and set, both, the employer and the employees can better understand their role in the activity and can reach to the goal effectively and efficiently.

(2) **Setting Performance Standards:** Once the parameters are set, the next step is to identify the performance standards. Performance standards are nothing but analysing and finalising the expected level of performance. This is decided in advance so that gaps, if any, can be corrected at the earliest.

(3) **Planning Performance of all Constituents:** As we have seen in earlier points, performance management activities involve continuous improvement of all the processes and people in the organisation. So after setting the performance standards, to get the desired results, it is imperative to mould the behaviour and performance of the employees in a particular way so that it generates the preferred output.

(4) **Identifying Competencies / Competency Gaps:** When we are in the process of moulding the behaviour of the employees, it is important that we understand the competency gaps if any. Gaps are nothing but a space between standard competencies and expected competencies. Once it is identified that there are gaps, these can be healed with the help of training and development programmes.

(5) **Planning Performance Development Activities:** To bridge the gaps between standard and actual performance, performance development activities are planned in the organisation. These activities are in the form of on-the-job training, management games, case studies, outbound training etc.

(6) **Creating Ownership:** This is one of the most important aspects in the entire performance management initiative. Until and unless the employees feel that they are the owners of their organisation and their smallest leap of step is going to affect the organisation in either a positive or negative way, they will not behave in an expected manner.

(7) **Recognising and Promoting Performance Culture:** It is very important that the employees become used to performing better. If the organisation follows performance culture, every employee would be performance oriented and there are minimal chances of dissatisfaction, errors, and wastages among the employees.

1.1.7 Historical Developments in Performance Management

Performance Management is most often used in the workplace, and applies where people interact such as school, colleges, community meetings, sports teams, governmental agencies, etc., which has evolved positively over a period of time. Let us look at the historical development of performance management.

The term performance management gained its importance from the times when the competitive pressures in the market started rising and the organisations felt the need of introducing a comprehensive performance management process into their system for improving the overall productivity and performance effectiveness. Performance Management is about the success of individuals in their jobs, making the best use of their abilities, realising their full potential and ensuring their alignment to the corporate agenda, thereby maximising their contribution to the success of the organisation.

1. **First Phase:** The origin of performance management can be traced to the early 1960s when the performance appraisal systems were in practice. During this period, **Annual Confidential Reports (ACRs)** were maintained for controlling the behaviours of the employees and these reports provided substantial information on the performance of the employees. Any negative comment or feedback would have a very serious impact on the career path of the employees. The remarks of these reports were never communicated to the employees, and strict confidentiality was always maintained. There was absence of transparent mechanism for feedback and communication. This system suffered from a lot of drawbacks.

2. **Second Phase:** This phase continued from late 1960s till early 1970s. The drawbacks of the first phase were removed to some extent during this phase. The feedback / ratings received by the employees were communicated to them so that they take some corrective actions to improve their performance. The employees usually used to get a formal written communication on their identified areas of improvements if the rating for any specific trait used to be below 33%.

3. **Third Phase:** In this phase, the term ACR was replaced by performance appraisal. One of the key changes introduced during the year was that the employees were permitted to write down their accomplishments in confidential performance reports. The employees were allowed to write about their accomplishments in the self-appraisal form in the end of the year. In spite of these changes, the entire process was control oriented rather than development oriented.

4. **Fourth Phase:** This phase started in the mid 1970s and its origin was in India as the great business tycoons like Larsen and Toubro introduced appreciable reforms in this field. The appraisal process during this phase was more development driven. The system focused on performance planning, review and development of an employee by undertaking transparent and methodical approach.

This phase was a warm change in the area of performance management.

1.1.8 Advantages

(1) **Performance Based Conversations:** Managers get busy with day-to-day responsibilities and often neglect the necessary interactions with staff that provide the opportunity to coach and offer performance feedback. A performance management process forces managers to discuss performance issues with employees. It is this consistent coaching that affects changed behaviours and employee development.

(2) **Targeted Staff Development:** If done well, a good performance management system can be a positive way to identify developmental opportunities and can be an important part of a succession planning process. All employees are on a development journey and it is the organisation's responsibility to be preparing them for increased responsibility.

(3) **Encouragement to Staff:** Performance appraisals should be a celebration of all the wonderful things an employee does over the course of a year and should be an encouragement to staff. There should be no surprises if issues are addressed as they arise and not held until the annual review.

(4) **Rewards Staff for a Job Well Done:** If pay increases and/or bonuses are tied to the performance appraisal process, staff can see a direct correlation between performance and financial rewards. This motivates and encourages employees to perform at higher levels.

(5) **Under-performers Identified and Eliminated:** As hard as we try, it is inevitable that some employees just won't cut the mustard as they say. An effective performance appraisal process can help identify and document underperformers, allowing for a smooth transition if the relationship needs to be terminated.

(6) **Documented History of Employee Performance:** It is very important that all organisations keep a performance record of all employees. This is a document that should be kept in the employee's HR file.

(7) **Allows for Employee Growth:** Motivated employees value structure, development and a plan for growth. An effective performance management system can help an employee reach their full potential and this is positive for both the employee and manager. A good manager takes pride in watching an employee grow and develop professionally.

Organisations should take a global look at their performance management system and have very objective goals that are tied to strategic initiatives and the performance management process. Successful organisations have learned the secret to this and while not always perfect, a constant striving to improve the process can help organisations reach their vision.

1.1.9 Disadvantages

(1) **Time Consuming:** It is recommended that a manager spend about an hour per employee writing performance appraisals and depending on the number of people being evaluated, it can take hours to write the department's PA but also hours meeting with staff to review the PA.

(2) **Discouragement:** If the process is not a pleasant experience, it has the potential to discourage staff. The process needs to be one of encouragement, positive reinforcement and a celebration of a year's worth of accomplishments. It is critical that managers document not only issues that need to be corrected, but also the positive things an employee does throughout the course of a year, and both should be discussed during a PA.

(3) **Inconsistent Message:** If a manager does not keep notes and accurate records of employee behaviour, they may not be successful in sending a consistent message to the employee. We all struggle with memory with as busy as we all are so it is critical to document issues (both positive and negative) when it is fresh in our minds so we have it to review with the employee at performance appraisal time.

(4) **Biases:** It is difficult to keep biases out of the PA process and it takes a very structured objective process and a mature manager to remain unbiased through the process. Performance appraisal rater errors are common for managers who assess performance so understanding natural biases is important to fair evaluations.

1.2 Performance Appraisal Vs. Performance Management

The terms 'performance management' and 'performance appraisal' are sometimes used synonymously, but they are different. Performance management is a comprehensive, continuous and flexible approach to the management of organisations, teams and individuals which involves the maximum amount of dialogue between those concerned. Performance appraisal is a more limited approach which involves managers making top-down assessments and rating the performance of their subordinates at an annual performance appraisal meeting.

Points of Difference	Performance Appraisal	Performance Management
System	It is a formal system of review and evaluation of individual or team performance.	It is a goal-oriented system to ensure that organisational processes exist to maximise the productivity of employees, teams and ultimately the organisation.
Time span	It is a periodic event to reflect and evaluate past performance.	It is an ongoing organisational process that is conducted to maximise the productivity of employees.
Objective	Its main objective is to identify strengths and weaknesses of an employee's performance and to discover developmental goals.	Its main objective is of improving the organisation's effectiveness.
Focus	It is mainly focused on the individual's past mistakes and misbehaviours.	It is mainly focused on individual's growth.
Linking	It is linked to financial rewards.	Can be linked to total rewards.
Perspective	It has an individualistic perspective.	It has a holistic perspective.
Concentrated upon	Largely concentrated upon quantitative aspects of performance.	Largely concentrated upon qualitative aspects of performance.
Nature	It is rigid and inflexible in nature.	It is flexible and adaptable in nature.
Goal-setting	Goal setting is done for short to mid-run goals.	Goal setting is done for long-run goals.
Approach	Its approach is operational.	Its approach is strategic.
Ratings	Use of ratings.	Ratings less common.
Ownership	Owned by the HR department.	Owned by line managers.

Here is the graphical view of the major differences between the two processes:

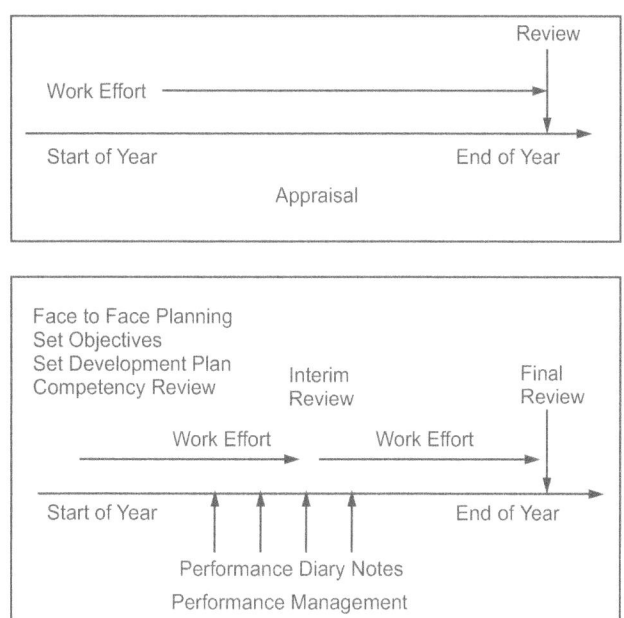

Fig 1.2: Differences between Performance Management and Performance Appraisal

1.3 Performance Management Vs. Human Resource Management

Both the terms refer to one and the same function of management and that is managing the people at work. However, Human Resource Management is mainly focussed on best utilising the man power by understanding their strengths and weaknesses and engaging them in different occupations so that their productivity can be increased. Therefore, training and development and employee engagements are part of it. Personnel Management, on the other hand, is mainly concerned with maintaining good employee- employer relationship and activities connected with it. Therefore, Personnel Management mainly works around Industrial/ Employee/ Labour Relations and activities connected with grievance handling, negotiations, enforcement of labour statutes, looking after welfare of employees and so on.

Basis of Difference	Personnel Management (PM)	Human Resource Management (HRM)
Strategic nature	Predominantly dealing with day-to-day issues. Ad-hoc and reactive in nature: a short-term perspective rather than strategic.	Dealing with day-to-day issues; but proactive in nature and integrated with other management functions. A deliberately long-term, strategic view of human resources.
Psychological contract	Based on compliance on the part of the employee.	Based on seeking willing commitment of the employee.
Job Design	Typically Tayorlist / Fordist.	Typically team based.
Organisational structure	Hierarchical Tendency to vertical integration.	Flexible with core of key employees surrounded by peripheral shells. High degree of outsourcing.
Remuneration	Collective base rates 'Pay by position' Any additional bonuses linked to Taylorist work systems.	Market-based. Individual and/or team performance. 'Pay for contribution'.
Recruitment	Sophisticated recruitment practices for senior staff only. Strong reliance on external local labour market for most recruitment.	Sophisticated recruitment for all employees. Strong internal labour market for core employees. Greater reliance on external labour market for non-core.
Training/ development	Limited and usually restricted. to training non-managerial employees. Narrowly job-related. Management development limited to top executives and fast-track candidates.	Transformed into a learning. and development philosophy transcending job-related training. An ongoing developmental role for all core employees including non-management. Strong emphasis on management and leadership development. A learning organisation culture.

Employee relations perspective	Pluralist: collectivist; low trust.	Unitarist: individualistic; high trust.
Organisation of the function	Specialist/professional. Separated from line management. Bureaucratic and centralised.	Largely integrated into line management for day-to-day HR issues. Specialist HR group to advise and create HR policy.
Welfare role	Residual expectations.	No explicit welfare role.
Criteria for success of the function	Minimising cost of human resources.	Control of HR costs, but also maximum utilisation of human resources over the long term.

Source: adapted and developed from Guest (1987)

1.4 Process of Performance Management

In today's workplace, performance improvement and the role of performance management is an increasingly popular topic. Business pressures are ever increasing and organisations are now required to become even more effective and efficient, perform better on business strategies and do more with less in order to remain competitive. To make the employees competitive, a lot of efforts are taken by the organisation such as management development programmes and executive development programmes and a clear vision is set in front of the employees. This takes some time, as performance of the employees cannot be changed overnight and hence a simple process is followed in order to get the expected results.

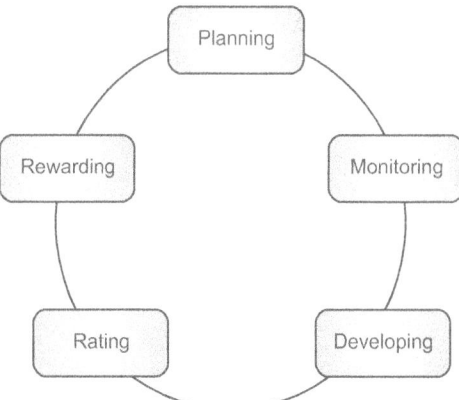

Fig 1.3: Performance Management Process

The process for performance management is as under:

1. Plan
2. Monitor
3. Develop
4. Rating
5. Rewarding

1. **Plan:** Planning is the first very basic step while an organisation is initiating for performance management. During this stage, the employer needs to plan the goals and objectives along with the employees and design a strategy for improving performance in order to attain the set objectives. This is a collaborative phase. And it is during this phase that the employer gets an opportunity to inform the employees about how their performance can impact the organisation. Planning is basically working in advance so that expectations and goals can be set.

2. **Monitor:** The manager needs to monitor the progress of the employees all round the year and not just during the performance review. This helps to identify and correct the errors at a very early stage and performance can be improved faster. It provides an opportunity for the supervisor to make the employees aware of their performance level whether favourable or unfavourable.

3. **Developing:** The manager should be able to decide by continuously monitoring the employees, whether the employees need additional development to achieve their assigned responsibilities. It is important to note that employee development does not only mean remediation but also enhancing good performance.

4. **Rating:** From time to time, organisations find it useful to summarise employee performance. This can be helpful for looking at and comparing performance over time or among various employees. Organisations need to know who their best performers are. Rating means evaluating employee performance against the elements and standards in an employee's performance plan and assigning a summary rating of record. The rating of record is assigned according to procedures included in the organisation's appraisal programme. It is based on the work performed during an entire appraisal period.

5. **Rewarding:** The manager must make meaningful distinction while granting rewards. The rewards should be clearly distinguishable across various performance levels and above. Performance Management must support compensation decisions.

1.5 Processes for Managing Performance

Process One: Performance Planning

Getting a performance management system up and running starts with proper planning. An organisation needs to ensure they have defined performance goals set in place before a performance period — that is, either after a performance appraisal or at the start of a new position.

In the planning phases, we need to guarantee that the goals are aligned with organisational goals. Once these goals are finalised they can be communicated directly to the employee.

One tip for creating goals is to include no more than three challenging, but attainable, goals. Defining three goals as the main focus is enough for employees to work towards. More than three challenging goals can be overwhelming and stressful. Although some positions will be an exception, try to remain fair and review the responsibilities of the position carefully before creating an employee's goals.

The manager's role is to encourage employees and ensure that they are provided with the resources and help needed to overcome any obstacles in the period of a performance review.

Process Two: Ongoing Feedback

Once the performance period has started, this is the time for organisations to provide ongoing support and monitoring to keep employees on the right track. Managers should be available to provide regular feedback about the behaviours and results discussed in the planning phase. To be effective, managers should provide candid feedback, focusing on behaviours rather than traits, along with productive discussions on how to improve. For further effectiveness, these conversations should take place routinely and informally through follow-up meetings. Employees should be encouraged to seek feedback and bring up any issues that arise during the performance period.

Process Three: Employee Input

As the performance period is coming to an end and prior to the formal performance appraisal process, ask employees for their input and their experience, achievements, and thoughts on their performance. These can be considered in the evaluation process. Good performance management is a joint collaboration between employees and the organisation — including employees in the process will increase their participation, as well as their understanding of their importance and influence in the organisation.

Process Four: Performance Evaluation

Conducting the performance evaluation is the key to the whole performance management process and should be allowed ample time and resources to be completed. The actual employee evaluation measure should focus on five to ten behavioural dimensions (or whatever appropriate number of dimensions, depending on the position).

Behavioural dimensions should follow this structure:

(i) Be related to organisational goals.

(ii) Be derived from a review of the competencies needed to perform the specific job.

(iii) If the competencies needed are unknown or unclear, a job analysis can be conducted.

(iv) A job analysis involves systematically gathering information about the job through reviewing job descriptions, interviewing employees, observing employees doing the job and other methods.

Once the behaviour dimensions to be included in the performance evaluation are established, performance criteria can be determined.

For example, in a customer service position, the competency of handling customer complaints may be evaluated on a scale, such as: 1 (exceeds expectations), 2 (meets expectations), and 3 (below expectations).

Descriptions of the specific behaviours associated with each of these would be provided to the manager rating the employees — meaning each level of performance should be clearly defined. While creating the performance criteria can be difficult, it's important to focus on the results, i.e. whether the employees succeeded in delivering the bottom-line, and also how the employee performed to deliver this bottom-line.

Process Five: Performance Review

The last stage of the performance management process is where most of the hard work that has gone into the performance period can be seen and understood. During the performance review, results of the performance appraisal are discussed, and the manager and employee make plans for improvement through developmental strategies. Managers discuss the ratings with the employees, giving specific feedback regarding the rationale behind the ratings.

To facilitate development and increase employee performance, managers can use "Developmental Handbooks." These handbooks consider each competency that is covered in the performance appraisal process. For each competency specific, developmental activities are described. These include formal training programmes available to employees, books, websites, as well as on-the-job and other developmental activities that will help them to improve in that competency.

Finally, managers should not discuss consequences of the performance appraisal associated with compensation at this meeting. This meeting is solely for the purpose of review and discussing the employee's performance and steps for future development. Instead, a separate meeting should be allocated to discuss any implications for pay, promotion, or other consequences.

1.6 Essence of Performance Management

A Performance Management programme may not always improve performance, however it largely tries to open up the opportunities to improve the company's profitability. A large majority of managers and other employees agree that their performance management programmes do not improve business results. A recent study conducted by McKinsey & Company suggests that only 30 percent of employees say they receive feedback of real value in improving their performance. A performance management programme may not always improve performance and only such companies are among a small minority of global companies.

Typically the essence of a performance management system is as under:

- To review the performance of the employees over a given period of time and taking steps to manage it further.
- To judge the gap between actual and standard performance.
- To help the management in exercising organisational control.
- To diagnose the training and development needs of the future.
- To provide information to assist in HR decisions like promotions, transfer etc.
- Provide clarity of the expectations and responsibilities of the functions to be performed by the employees.
- To judge the effectiveness of the other human resource functions of the organisation such as recruitment, selection, training and development.
- To reduce the grievances of the employees.
- Helps to strengthen the relationship and communication between superior–subordinates and management – employees.

According to a recent survey, the percentage of organisations using performance management for the following purposes is shown in the figure below:

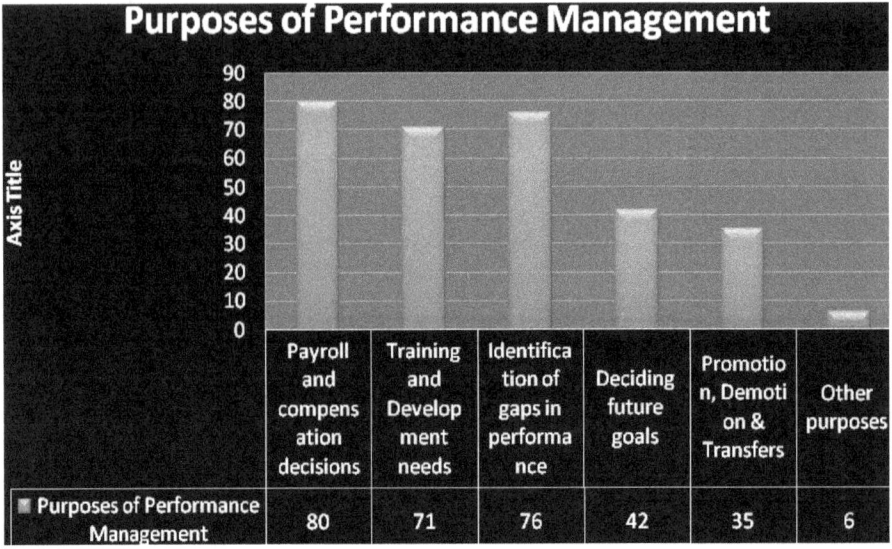

Fig 1.4: The percentage of organisations using Performance Management

The most significant reasons of using performance management are:

- Making payroll and compensation decisions – 80%
- Training and development needs – 71%
- Identifying the gaps between desired and actual performance and their causes – 76%
- Deciding future goals and course of actions – 42%
- Promotions, demotions and transfers – 49%
- Other purposes – 6% (Including job analysis, and providing superior support, assistance and counselling.)

1.7 Implications of Performance Management

The nature of organisations and the structure of jobs are changing rapidly, and many of these changes have implications for performance management. Two examples of the many changes occurring at the organisational level are:

1. The increasing "flattening" of many companies through the elimination of layers of management, and
2. The "rebuilding" process after major organisational restructuring, through which organisations report a new or renewed commitment to specific values, such as customer service.

The first trend is relevant to performance evaluation because there are fewer people in the management positions to evaluate performance. Those managers who remain often have responsibility for a larger number of employees and often have many other responsibilities, and within flatter organisations many employees have more discretion over the way they perform their jobs, which makes it harder for a manager to recognise performance issues and problems through observation.

- The majority of performance management programmes are driven by the need to arrive at a rating used to determine the size of the employee merit increases and, in some cases, incentive awards. As a result, many supervisors determine the amount of merit increase they believe is adequate to retain and reward employees, then use company guidelines to support it into a performance rating that justifies the desired increase.
- Another common use is to make termination and promotion decisions. In fact, the bulk of the supervisor's effort is arriving at a judgement of performance. Employees, of course, are likely to contest that judgement unless they are rated at a high performance level. As a result, the focus on improving individual performance is displaced by the focus on judging and rewarding.
- The focus of most performance management programmes is on individuals, not teams. Team performance is not typically considered in most performance feedback. People and Their Jobs: What's Real, What's Rhetoric? Rating the performance of individuals alone often results in destructive competition and conflict among team members. Given how frequently people work in teams these days, the focus on individuals is outdated and often counter-productive.

Performance management should be based on the complete details, facts and events taking place throughout the year which needs continuous monitoring and checks through various means. Such need for details can lead to micromanagement by the superiors. Apart from limiting the employee's growth and learning, micromanagement also hinders healthy superior subordinate relationships and eventually the manager's career development. Therefore, a better idea would be periodic discussions and feedback based on the overall performance of the employees and the results achieved.

Points to Remember

- Performance Management is both a strategic and integrated approach to delivering successful results in the organisation by improving the performance and developing the capabilities of teams and individuals.

- Performance management is an ongoing process of communication between a supervisor and an employee that occurs throughout the year, in support of accomplishing the strategic objectives of the organisation.
- The concerns of Performance Management are as under:
  1. Concerned with the output
  2. Concerned with the measurement of results
  3. Concerned with planning
  4. Concerned with continuous improvement
  5. Concerned with establishing appropriate culture
  6. Concerned with the provision of procedural fairness and transparency in the process of decision making.
- Scope of Performance Management
  1. Identifying performance parameters
  2. Setting performance standards
  3. Planning performance of all constituents
  4. Identifying competencies
  5. Planning Performance development activities
  6. Creating ownership
  7. Recognising and promoting performance culture
- The terms 'performance management' and 'performance appraisal' are sometimes used synonymously, but they are different. Performance management is a comprehensive, continuous and flexible approach to the management of organisations, teams and individuals which involves the maximum amount of dialogue between those concerned. Performance appraisal is a more limited approach which involves managers making top-down assessments and rating the performance of their subordinates at an annual performance appraisal meeting.
- The process for performance management is as under:
  1. Plan
  2. Monitor
  3. Develop
  4. Rating
  5. Rewarding

Questions for Discussion

1. Write a short note on concerns and implications of Performance Management.
2. Explain in detail the process of Managing Performance.
3. What do you mean by Performance Management? Explain the scope of Performance Management.
4. Explain the Evolution of Performance Management.
5. What are the differences between Performance Management and Performance Appraisal?
6. What are the differences between Performance Management and Human Resource Management?

Project Questions

1. To whom do you think a Performance Management System is significant to the organisation or the individual? Justify. What strategies do you suggest while developing and implementing system for performance management?
2. You are the Zonal Marketing head of a FMCG Company. One of your subordinates has been by-passed for promotion due to non-achievement of targets. He fears loss of job to follow the loss of status due to non-promotion. However, two years ago, he was in achievers, and a very sincere subordinate. How would you counsel him so that he is able to deliver his best for the company?

Chapter 2...

Performance Management Process

Contents ...

- 2.1 Introduction
- 2.2 Performance Planning: Setting Objectives
  - 2.2.1 Types of Objectives
  - 2.2.2 Key Concerns of a Performance Management System
  - 2.2.3 Organisational and Individual Performance Plans
  - 2.2.4 Components of Manager's Performance and Development Plans
  - 2.2.5 Setting Mutual Expectations and Performance Criteria
- 2.3 Performance Managing
  - 2.3.1 Objectives of Performance Managing
  - 2.3.2 Process of Performance Managing
  - 2.3.3 Importance of Performance Management
- 2.4 Performance Appraisal
  - 2.4.1 Objectives of Performance Appraisal
  - 2.4.2 Performance Appraisal Process
  - 2.4.3 Types of Performance Appraisal
  - 2.4.4 Achieving Effective Performance Appraisal
- 2.5 Monitoring and Mentoring
  - 2.5.1 Introduction
  - 2.5.2 Importance of Monitoring
  - 2.5.3 Role of Mentor in the Organisation
  - 2.5.4 Supervision
  - 2.5.5 Objectives of Monitoring Performance
  - 2.5.6 Principles of Monitoring
  - 2.5.7 Monitoring Process
- 2.6 Periodic Reviews
- 2.7 Problem Solving in Performance Management
- 2.8 Engendering Trust in Performance Management
- 2.9 Role Efficacy
  - Points to Remember
  - Questions for Discussion
  - Project Questions

Learning Objectives ...

- To be able to understand performance planning and setting objectives involving organisational and individual performance plans, components of manager's development plan and setting mutual expectations and performance criteria
- To understand the objectives, process and importance of performance managing
- To explain the objectives, process of performance appraisal, types and guidelines for achieving effective performance appraisal
- To discuss the objectives, principles and process of monitoring
- To understand the concepts of periodic reviews, problem solving, engendering trust and role efficacy relating to performance management

2.1 Introduction

Performance management is the most critical activity in the organisation. If not done properly, the organisation will not be able to achieve its strategic objectives of profit maximisation and growth. If the performance of all the employees is directed towards a single objective, a harmony can be achieved in all the processes. To reach up to this standard, organisations need to state and communicate very clearly the performance standards set for the employees. After communicating the performance standards it must be clearly followed that the performance of the employees is carefully monitored and constructive feedback is shared on the same. Conducting regular appraisals is also a part of performance management activity.

Performance management is a very integrative activity, wherein all the employees of the organisation are brought together and their performance is regulated towards the accomplishment of organisational goals.

Employee performance management system includes:

- Getting the work plan ready and setting performance standards
- Closely monitoring the performance
- Developing the potential of the people to perform
- Periodically reviewing the performance of the employees
- Providing appropriate reward to the high performing employees

By setting a process of performance management, the employees understand what exactly they need to produce in order to help the organisation in the accomplishment of its goals and objectives.

An Effective Performance Management Process (PMP):
- Increases the employee involvement, development and feedback mechanism.
- Is constant across various units and departments in the organisation in order to have optimum utilisation of the human and other resources.
- It is always flexible, extremely fair and transparent and easily understood by all.
- Always tries to align the individual goals to the organisation's vision and mission statement.
- Plans for strong succession planning in the organisation.
- Clearly defines the relationship of the employees with the organisation from the time they are recruited in the organisation to their exit.
- Constantly involves and develops the employees throughout the year
- Establishes performance goals and encourages employees to meet performance goals.
- Gives authority to the supervisors in providing fair and consistent feedback on performance of the employees.
- Includes past performance review as the basis of measuring current and future performance of the employees.

The basic objective of any performance management process is to develop the performance of the employee as a whole, then of the team, then of the department and finally of the organisation. It acts as an instrument that plays a vital role in changing the culture of the organisation and makes it a high performance work culture. Its main objective is to meet and develop the capabilities of people and discover their potentialities for the benefit of themselves and of the organisation. It always gives the chance for self-development and at the same time it also makes the superiors responsible for guiding and monitoring the performance of the employees.

2.2 Performance Planning: Setting Objectives

Failing to plan is planning to fail. This sums up the importance of the planning part of the performance management process. Effective performance planning is the critical first phase of performance management. If done well, it can set up people and thus the organisation to succeed.

Before one gets to 'performing', it is important to get down to 'planning' what is to be done. Planning of performance begins with the setting of objectives. In its simplest form, objective setting is the process by which corporate objectives are broken down into deliverables for functions/business units, departmental teams and then individuals.

2.2.1 Types of Objectives

- To motivate the employees towards superior level of performance. When the employees are motivated and committed towards their work, they need little supervision and tend to perform their work on their own. This makes the employees more independent and helps understand the goals and objectives in a much clearer way. In this way, the organisation as well employees grows at the same pace.

- To help the employees understand the knowledge, skills, and attitudes for enhancing their own performance level for the growth and development of self and organisation. It is very important for the employees to know what level of knowledge and skills they possess. Only when they are fully aware of it, they can develop it further. Hence actual performance is needed to be known in order to achieve the standards. Performance management process always helps employees know their current position and at the same time prepare them to take up future challenges.

- Boosting the morale of the employees for achieving high performance levels and thereby achieving high rewards for their performance, in short setting the performance based reward system in the organisation. It is always observed that employees will not work up to the mark till the time they understand what they are going to get in return.

Hence a reward system is introduced in the organisation and it is purposefully linked with the performance management process. When employees come to know about a specific reward that will be given to them once they achieve the desired level of performance, they tend to become more confident, committed and involved. This helps the employees to enjoy their work and reap the benefits and the organisation is benefitted with more output and happier employees.

- Setting a strong two-way communication system between the employees and their supervisors is important. Having a clear dialogue between the two helps the employee to understand the expectations of the organisation from him/her and how far he/she has been able to achieve the same. Communication plays a vital role in any process in the organisation. Whatever plans and goals that management has in mind towards the growth and development of the employees must be communicated to the employees as they are the executors of the plan.

Once it is clear that employees and the management are looking at the same goal in the same way, it helps to strengthen the process in a great way. Employees in such regards need very little supervision and percentage of mistakes is also lowered due to clear understanding of the expectations.

- Strong communication system as regard performance management helps early detection of performance inefficiencies. Thus, when an inefficiency is detected at an early stage it can be overcome through constant monitoring, mentoring and informal talks. As discussed in the earlier point, a strong communication system is an integral part of the performance management process. It is imperative to make the performance standards clear to the employees which will not only help them to do their work efficiently but will also help the organisation to measure the performance of the employees.
- Encouraging personal growth and career advancement are the basis of the performance management process. This is a very important aspect of the performance management process. It is designed in such a way that it promotes personal growth and career advancement along with organisational growth and development. When the employees realise that they are growing along with the organisation, they feel happier and tend to work even more for further growth and development.

2.2.2 Key Concerns of a Performance Management System

- It is extremely result oriented and hence concerned with results, output in terms of knowledge gained and applied, skills learned and utilised and the desired level of output is produced or not etc. Having a result oriented performance management system is a very important aspect at the organisational level. When the process focuses on getting desired results and makes the employees work in a particular way fetches a huge amount of success for the organisation and at the same time it makes sure that the employees are motivated enough to work towards the desired results.
- It is concerned with the measurement of performance and aligning it with the goals of the organisation for consistent growth. This is a very critical aspect of performance management. When the system measures the performance, it gives a clear idea to the management about how the employees are performing, where do they stand as far as their performance is concerned and what needs to be done to bridge the gap between actual and standard level of performance. The performance management system provides a scope for constant measurement of the performance and at the same time, aligns the performance of the employees to the organisational performance as a whole so that complete growth and development can be achieved.
- It is concerned with setting the business objectives much in advance for the smooth conduct of operations. Having objectives set well in advance provides a clear picture to the employees as to what is expected out of them and what level of performance do they need to show. By having the objectives set, performance measurement and

then management becomes extremely easy and scientific, as management can any time go back and alter the objectives suiting the current requirements of the market, organisation, and individuals. This ensures smooth working and carrying out of the process in the organisation.

- Always striving for continuous improvement and bringing about change in all the processes of the organisation for creating and developing the culture of performance. The main idea behind having a performance management system in the organisation is to change the way employees are performing at the moment. As it is very well known to all that change is the only constant and we all have to change with the change in order to sustain against competition. And the employees can only survive in the market when they have adequate skills, right attitude and upgraded knowledge. This is possible with an extremely competitive performance management system. The system constantly checks for the performance loop and if there are any obstacles or grey areas in the performance of the employees, it provides scope for improving the performance of the employees for the growth and development of the organisation.

- It is concerned with setting the culture of performance and along with that culture of openness, confrontation, trust, authenticity, proactive, autonomy, collaboration, experimentation. If the culture has these dimensions, the performance system can be implemented very quickly and effectively. As was discussed in the earlier points, the performance management system of the organisation must always be aligned with the processes and practices present in the organisation in order to achieve overall growth and development performance management system must always try to bring about such a culture that it accepts the changing and growing knowledge and skills of the employees and at the same time motivates employees to perform even better every time.

- It is concerned with the provisions related to decision making while giving rewards and remuneration to the employees. Trust builds performance and performance leads to success, growth and expansion of the business unit. The main idea behind having a performance management system is to make the employees independent as far as work, output and performance are concerned. When employees come to know that their performance is going to be complimented with appropriate rewards and recognitions, they tend to perform with utmost care and precaution. They tend to concentrate more on their work and need very little supervision. This makes them much better at the decision making. And their dependency on their supervisors reduces.

2.2.3 Organisational and Individual Performance Plans

Most organisations review their performance in terms of "effectiveness" and the amount of revenue generated for a particular time frame but there is more to performance management than this. To make the performance management effort an effective one, there needs to be a synergy between individual and organisational goals.

When it comes to performance management systems, organisation and employees become two separate entities. The performance of the employees and the performance of the organisation as a whole must complement each other in order to get ahead towards the achievement of set goals and objectives. By improving the performance of the employees will not guarantee the change in the working of organisation or it will not affect the organisation in any way. On the other hand, if the plans are made for organisation as well as employees, both can function effectively and goals achievement becomes easier.

Hence, a performance management system provides for creation of separate plans for the organisation and for the employees, wherein the nature of objectives is different for both of them but the expected output is related to each other. When the efforts of the organisation and the employees are coordinated, the results can be achieved in less time and with fewer errors.

Thus, organisational performance plans and employees' performance plans must be made separately and progress of the both must be recorded timely.

2.2.4 Components of Manager's Performance and Development Plans

Performance management systems need to be implemented for managers as well. Managers are the ones who develop employees and help them achieving personal as well as organisational goals. Given below are the components of a manager's performance and development plans:

1. **Ascertaining Performance Development Needs:** Before implementing any plan in the organisation, it must be ensured that it caters to the needs of the managers. The needs of the managers can be ascertained by taking into consideration the kind of role they play, the level of responsibility that they possess and the skills that they require to move ahead in the organisational structure and also in their career.

    Managers are the ones who share the performance plans with other employees working in the organisation. Hence great care must be taken while planning for performance management activity for them. The goals set for them must include improving the performance of the employees working under them, providing timely and honest performance feedback to the employees etc. The manager can be successful only when he understands the performance needs of the organisation. As they will help him plan for the performance management activities for the employees as well as self. Once these needs are properly assessed, the appropriate plan can be designed for the performance development of managers.

2. **Appraisal of Present Management Talent:** This is the most important component of a manager's performance development plan. In this step, the potential of the managers is assessed and their current skills level is identified. Then the output is matched with the standard set by the organisation and gaps, if any, in the performance are then covered with the help of management development techniques present in the organisation.

   Appraisal of present management talent is very much needed if the organisation wants to be strong performance wise. When the performance of the managers is assessed and rewarded, the managers feel confident about the skills and knowledge they possess at the moment and also motivate them to perform even better in the next assessment cycle. Appraisal of performance always provides positive motivation to the individual and promises improved level of performance during the next appraisal cycle.

3. **Planning of Individual Development Programme:** The performance needs of each individual are different because basically each person is different from the other. Hence the performance need of each individual must be assessed carefully so that he can contribute to the overall growth and development of the organisation effectively. On the basis of individual needs assessment, developmental programmes are scheduled and conducted.

   The performance of the organisation and of the individual must be planned, managed and assessed independently. This helps the organisation understand what level of performance do the employees display and what improvements they must demonstrate in order to grow and develop further. Individual development programme also provides a platform for the employees to understand their own strengths and weaknesses and also gives them a chance to improve their grey areas and develop the strong points. It thus becomes easier for the management to assess the performance needs of the individual and appropriate training can be provided to them for betterment of the performance.

4. **Competency based Performance Training:** For managers it is very essential to have competency approach attached. Because at the managerial level enhancement of competencies is very much needed rather than just skills development. For managers it is more about competencies rather than skills and attitudes. Hence they are presented with a basket of competencies and their performance is managed alongside the competencies that they are expected to possess.

When the managers develop required competencies at work, they can better groom the employees working under them. Hence competency based performance management system must be implemented in the organisation especially for the managers. At the same time, proper training must be given to them so that they better understand their roles and can grasp whatever is being taught to them and implement the same at their work.

2.2.5 Setting Mutual Expectations and Performance Criteria

Management training explains how to establish, write and communicate clear job performance expectations in an effective manner in order to create a solid foundation for performance appraisal. The basis of performance appraisal will not be set until and unless the performance expectations are not clear to employees as well as employers. Without proper job expectations, employees will not be able to understand what their priorities are and how to invest their efforts, how to utilise free time that they get, and how to avoid unnecessary stress coming out of work. Given below are the points that help in setting mutual expectations.

Managers	Employees
Plan and manage the performance of the employees.	Understand how their performance affects the outcomes of other departments and their contribution in the overall development of the organisation.
Communicate the goals to the employees along with their responsibilities.	Understanding the goals and asking for clarifications if any goal is unclear to them. And constantly work on the goal assigned to them.
Foster a working environment that encourages employee participation.	Be a part of performance planning process. Be proactive in nature and provide valuable inputs in the decision making system.
Provide regular, constructive and timely feedback to the employees.	Taking the feedback positively and work upon improving the problem areas, if any.
Monitor the performance of the employees throughout the year.	Get the performance assessed and check how far they are able to achieve the performance goals.
Help, guide and coach the employees wherever needed.	Be open and transparent about professional growth and development.

2.3 Performance Managing

Performance managing is *a systematic process of establishing shared performance goals for the employees in the organisation regarding what needs to be achieved, how it is to be achieved, when it is to be achieved etc*. It is all about aligning the performance of the employees to the organisational objectives and strategies. The main focus of a performance management system is on improving the performance of the employees through constant monitoring of the performance and providing remedial measures.

Every organisation wants to be in the competition and ultimately beat the competition and stay number one in the market. When any organisation reaches to the top position in the market, it automatically earns goodwill and a lot of reputation for itself. It leads to increased market share and consequently creation of high performance work systems. To enhance the overall performance of the organisation, high performing employees are required at the organisation. Having high performers in the organisation ensures high productivity, an engaged and committed workforce, retention of talented employees etc.

When the employees in the organisation are not performing up to the mark, the organisation is likely to have frustrated customers, decreasing business productivity, and high turnover. This definitely leads to downward movement of the organisation. Which ultimately results into closing down of the organisation? To avoid this it must be noted that in order to make the organisation survive for as long as possible, it must have high performing employees in the team. And to make the employees high performing, there must be a process designed for managing and improving the performance of the employees.

Management of the performance is a very essential task in the organisation. If the organisation wants its employees to grow and develop further, it is very essential that it takes certain measures to management and improve the current level of performance possessed by the employees. There is a process set for performance management and improvement. It is very true that the performance of the employees cannot be changed overnight and it really takes a lot of time to improve the current level of performance to the standard level of performance. Hence each step defined in the performance management process must be carried out critically and effectively. If the employees are facing any difficulty while carrying out the goals set for them, the management must take efforts to clarify the doubts or alter the process if the need be.

2.3.1 Objectives of Performance Managing

1. **Increase Two Way Communication:** Performance managing is a system that involves both the employee and employer sitting together to discuss mutual performance goals for a particular period of time. This process makes the communication between the supervisor and employee clearer. The employees can

discuss their queries with the supervisor as many times as they can, as this is a mutual goal setting process. Also supervisors involve the employees in the goal setting in order to give more clarity and maintain transparency in the process. This way an employee gets a bigger picture as to what the organisation is expecting from them.

Setting the communication process always helps the organisation to gain cooperation from the employees, as the employees better understand what the management is facing at the moment and what is expected out of them in a particular situation. Hence a strong communication system must be present in the organisation in order to enhance the performance management and improvement initiative in the organisation.

2. **Identify and Resolve Performance Problems:** Performance management system has a provision for giving feedback to the employees through constant monitoring and checking. Constant review and monitoring of the performance helps early detection of performance problems and where the goal achievement is going wrong or where the employees are facing problems. Once this is identified at an early stage, offering solutions becomes very easy and hence the employees are able to achieve their performance goals quickly and in a systematic way.

   Identification of problem at an early stage is possible only when a strong communication system is present in the organisation, where employees can communicate the problems that they are facing while trying to improve their performance. Management here must listen to the problems stated by the employees and take remedial measures for the same. By taking immediately corrective action, the employees feel committed and their trust in the entire system of performance management increases.

3. **Recognise Quality Performance:** The way performance gaps are identified similarly, good performance can also be identified through performance management process. While the supervisor monitors the performance of the employees, he comes to know who is performing with dedication, who is a good performer of all and the supervisor can utilise such employees as an example to be kept in front of other employees in order to motivate them and encourage them to perform better. At the same time, good performed in the organisation can be easily rewarded to perform even better.

   It is very essential that the management recognises quality performance and appreciates it immediately. While trying for performance improvement, employees are looking for encouragement and approvals of their performance. When their performance is rewarded, they automatically feel satisfied and work with even more dedication. Hence rewarding and recognising quality performance at work is the first priority of the management in the performance management process.

4. **Providing Data for Administrative Purposes:** This is another objective of the performance management process. The data that is derived from managing the performance of the employees and the techniques during this process can be utilised for further use like for succession planning, performance linked benefits, rewards for performance etc. Without a performance management system it becomes difficult for the organisation to derive accurate data for further administrative purposes and decision making regarding couple of processes in the organisation. The data gathered during the performance management process is very critical and is used everywhere across an organisation.

As we all are aware that the functions and processes in the organisation are interdependent and hence the data gathered during performance management of the employees proves to be useful for other operations in the organisation. The purposes include salary administration, promotion, demotion, giving incentives and hikes, deciding designations, can be used during performance appraisal of the employees etc. Hence the data collected, observations, remarks made during the performance management process must be recorded properly so that they can be easily available when needed.

2.3.2 Process of Performance Managing

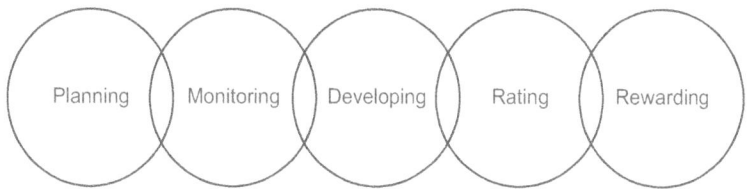

Fig. 2.1

1. **Planning:** To be an effective organisation, the work must be planned in advance. Planning is nothing but setting performance goals and expectations for the employees and communicating it to them in a clear manner in order to achieve organisational vision and mission statements. While planning for performance management, it is strongly recommended that people are involved in the planning process. This helps the employees understand what they need to do, why it is needed to be done, what are the consequences if they don't follow the plan and what are the remedial measures available.

The basic idea behind performance planning is establishing performance standards and conducting regular performance appraisal for the employees. Performance measurement standard must be specific, measurable, practical, verifiable, flexible, easy to understand and realistic. Through critical assessment, employees are held responsible for the work that was allotted to them and seen to it that they meet the expectations of the management. Employee performance management plans must be always flexible in order to make them work under any situation by just changing the primary objectives. When used effectively, performance planning data can be used for a number of appropriate uses.

2. **Monitoring:** The basis of performance management is having a check on the execution of the process continuously. Monitoring means checking the performance of the employees closely, providing them constructive and timely feedback and encouraging them to meet the established performance goals for them.

Monitoring the performance of the employees include regularly conducting performance review meetings, wherein the performance of the employees is compared against the standards and suggestions are provided to them in order to improve their performance for meeting the set goals. Continuous monitoring and feedback mechanism helps early detection of the errors and performance can be improved at a very early stage.

3. **Developing:** In order to improve the organisation performance wise, it is very much needed that the performance assessment needs are assessed and evaluated. Development in this context is developing the potential of the employees to perform better by providing training, development, case studies, management games, simulations, outbound training etc. Constantly developing the skills of the employees provides them tremendous confidence of performing the task with utmost care and improves their performance on the job. Improved performance leads to increased productivity and enhances job satisfaction they derive from the work. By conducting performance management process, development needs can be assessed systematically and timely. While planning and monitoring the work, the inefficiencies of the people on the job are easily identified at an early stage and can be corrected immediately to avoid heavy losses in the future.

4. **Rating:** It is useful for the organisation to analyse the performance of the employees and provide appropriate ratings. This data can be used further for various performances like comparing it with other employees to set performance standards. Organisations are constantly looking to know who their star performers are. In performance management process rating means evaluating the performance of the employees against the benchmark set and appropriate solutions are suggested for improving the current performance of the employees.

The performance data is achieved and while providing rating to the employees in this year, their past performance record is also taken into consideration. The rating is given as per the standard process set by the organisation. It is based on a specific time period during which the performance of the employees is assessed, monitored and developed. The rating is then associated with a number of benefits like salary hike, promotion, etc.

5. **Rewarding:** Rewarding is the last and the most important of all in the entire performance management process. Rewarding always encourages an employee to perform even better. Organisations nowaday's use rewards in both the ways i.e. positive reinforcement and negative reinforcement. It is called as the carrot and stick approach. While using this approach organisations try to motivate an employee by showing him the carrot of salary hike, growth, promotions, incentives etc. and make him/her perform in such a way that he/she becomes eligible for the rewards. At the same time, in order to keep the momentum, sometimes a stick is shown in the form of threatening them about losing the job, or lack of growth etc. Rewarding when used appropriately can do wonders for the employees.

2.3.3 Importance of Performance Management

Employees are an integral and the most critical part of the organisation. They help run the business smoothly and in an efficient manner. Out of this value and worth of the employees, the system of performance management has come into existence. Performance management does not only monitor the performance of the employees but also helps them enhance their capabilities by providing them feedback from time and time and up to the expectations of the organisation. Performance management allows the organisation to fully utilise the capabilities and potential of the employees. Let us now look at the importance of performance management process in the organisation.

The job market these days has become extremely dynamic and challenging in nature. It always wants employees who have updated knowledge and skills and a positive attitude towards the work. To create such employees it is very important and essential to improve their current level of performance to the expected level of performance. When their performance is improved, automatically there is a change in their attitude and behaviour. A motivated employee is not only good at his work but he also tries to encourage others, help others to get the desired level of output. Such kind of employees are wanted everywhere. Hence if performance management activity is taken seriously by all the organisations, they would be able to produce most competent, passionate and encouraged employees.

1. **Involving Employee in the Planning Stage:** Performance management provides an opportunity to the organisation to include the employees in the performance planning process. By setting the performance goals with the employees, the organisation gains a lot of advantage. This is so because management does not have to invest separate time in making the employees understand what goals are set for them and how they need to execute them. When the goal setting is happening

together, whatever doubts or confusion the employees have can be removed in the discussion and/or alternative solution to the problem can be identified.

By involving employees in the performance planning process, employees tend to perform more carefully as they know the importance and consequence of doing a particular task in a particular way and hence it increases the overall productivity of the employees. In a manufacturing company set-up it is also called as "workers participation in management". When the employees are involved in the performance management process right from the planning phase, they get a better understanding of what the organisation is expecting from a long term perspective. Once the vision and mission of the organisation is clear to the employees they tend to look at the work given to them with a larger perspective in mind. They start realising the impact the smallest mistake can have on the overall vision and mission of the organisation and they become more careful at their work. This promises superior performance of the employees and a more motivated workforce in the organisation.

2. **Monitoring the Progress of the Employees:** Having a performance management process set in the organisation, the performance of the employees can be managed in the most efficient, systematic and practical way. Monitoring the performance of the employees, the supervisors understand the run time problems that the employees are facing and appropriate solutions can be provided immediately. This reduces the lead time of understanding the problem and providing solutions. This makes the overall achievement of objectives very easy and at an early stage.

    Monitoring does not mean micro-management in the organisation but it simply includes checking the progress and performance of the employees regularly. In case of the performance management process, it is very essential to provide timely feedback to the employees. When the employees receive timely feedback they understand the seriousness of it. And necessary changes can be made at the earliest to avoid future losses.

3. **Ensuring All Round Development of the Employees:** The way an organisation has goals to achieve, employees also have certain goals to achieve other than what the organisation has set for them. Performance management process gives a chance to the employees to discover their hidden talents and strengths which can be utilised for the achievement of personal goals. And because of the strong process in existence where the feedback is provided on a regular basis, the employees feel free to share their performance progress and gaps, if any with their superiors. This creates a win-win situation across the organisation and performance management proves to be an important activity in the organisation.

Performance management process always aims at overall development of the employees and hence the programme is designed keeping in mind the strengths and weaknesses of the employees. The organisation must always focus on the development of the employees alongwith its own development and hence the employee should have personal as well as professional growth through the performance management process.

4. **Evaluation of Individual Performance:** Performance management is meant to be person specific. Each person has a different set of goals and objectives to achieve in relation to the strengths and weaknesses that he/she possesses. Evaluating the employees on individual basis is very essential for the growth and development of the organisation. Organisations can thus focus more on the improvement areas of the employees and at the same time enhancing their strong areas for generating the highest level of performance from them.

The overall development of the employee should be the main concern of the performance management process, similarly evaluation of the performance demonstrated by the employees must happen at regular intervals and most importantly, the feedback of the same must be shared with the employees as and when it is with the management. This helps the employees to improve their performance and meet the goals set by the organisation for them.

2.4 Performance Appraisal

Performance appraisal is a systematic evaluation of an individual's performance with respect to actual performance of the job and standard performance expected by the organisation. It is the assessment of an employee's performance in a systematic and transparent way. It is regarded as a developmental technique used for the all round development of employees. Performance assessment is based on past as well as potential performance of employees.

Performance appraisal is included in performance management or we can say that it is an important aspect of performance management. As we all know that the performance of the employees cannot be improved until and unless there is assessment and feedback sharing done by the management. Hence performance appraisal must be carried out with utmost care as the feedback shared under appraisal is going to be used as a stepping stone in deciding the performance management criteria for the individual.

2.4.1 Objectives of Performance Appraisal

1. **Promotions:** Performance appraisal data is used for promoting an employee in the organisation. Whether an employee is able to take up the higher positions in the

organisation or not can be identified only when the performance is assessed against the standards set for that position. Once the performance of the employee matches the standard performance or if the organisation recognises the potential of the employees to perform at higher levels, they can be easily promoted to the next level. Hence performance appraisal helps the organisation to promote an employee in the most systematic and proper way.

Promotion is liked by everyone and each employee has a dream or we can say has a career path to walk on. He always decides a particular designation for himself during his tenure with a particular organisation. By doing this, he plans his performance and tries to achieve the goals set for him by the organisation and whatever goals he has set for himself. This helps the management while promoting or demoting employees from a particular position. The actual performance of the employee is compared against the standard performance and if it satisfactory he is promoted to the next level in the hierarchy.

2. **Competency Building:** As performance appraisal identifies the potentialities of the employees, it helps the management to plan competency mapping and competency management programmes for the employees, since the output given by the employees do not necessarily state the competencies that each employee possesses. This helps the organisation to enhance the performance of the employees in a better way. Competency building is nothing but making the employee rich skills wise and knowledge wise.

Once the employee obtains desired level of competencies for doing a specific task, the objective of performance management is completed. The performance appraisal helps the management know what level of competencies does the employee possess and hence this data is used to design individual performance plans for a year for a particular employee.

3. **To Increase Motivation and Productivity:** Performance appraisal helps the employees to identify the skills necessary for them to achieve the set goals. When employees discover what it takes to be a better performer at the job, they are more motivated and enthusiastic to come to work every day and perform beyond their limits for meeting organisational as well as personal goals. This motivates the employees and also brings about a major change in their productivity levels. We all know that motivated employee tends to perform beyond his limits at the work. Organisations always want such employees working for it.

Performance appraisal and performance management must do this task of motivating the employees towards better performance each day. Appraisal process should be as transparent as possible and also managers should take care that they are free from biases as far as possible. The meaning of appraisal is assessing, recognizing the performance made by the employees and hence it must be done that way. Performance management later on must also focus on improving the morale and thereby productivity of the employee at work.

4. **To Retain Top Talent:** Retention has always been a critical issue for the organisation. Usually what happens is when an employee starts performing well he starts looking for suitable opportunities outside and ultimately leaves your organisation for an opportunity outside. To avoid this and reduce the rate of attrition, it is recommended that the performance of the employees is assessed closely, their hidden strengths are identified and they are provided with a conducive environment which will enable him to perform and remain committed to the organisation for the longer period of time.

   Retention is the biggest issue that organisations are facing today. Once the employees achieve specific skills, they tend to leave their jobs and join some other organisation for better prospects. And here the role of performance management begins. The process of managing and improving the performance must be such that it should increase the skills and knowledge of the employees and at the same time it should also focus on improving the commitment and belongingness of the employees towards the organisation.

5. **To Enhance Transparency:** Performance and development are very critical issues and must be handled with utmost care. Employees will not trust you and your process until each and every element in the process is crystal clear to them. Once they understand the process well and know that the process is true and fair, they tend to give their 100% for the overall achievement of the objectives set for the process, for the individual and organisation as a whole.

   Maintaining transparency in the process always gives a sense of confidence and trust to the employees. When the employees trust the process, the chance of better performance increases. The employees become more independent and remain active in the performance development process. The goals, vision, mission of the organisation must be shared with the employees during the performance improvement process. This helps the employees to understand the larger picture and their role in the overall performance improvement initiative.

2.4.2 Performance Appraisal Process

Given below is the process of performance appraisal:

1. **Preparation:** Every process in the organisation begins with planning. What results the organisation wants to achieve in this financial year must be ascertained. This helps the managers to set the goals for the team during a specific time period. Hence

planning for the performance appraisal process becomes the first step in the series. This helps in smooth operation of further processes of performance appraisal.

2. **Assessment:** On the basis of the plan set for the organisation during the year, there needs to be an assessment of performance, as there must be synergy between what the organisation expects and what employees are performing. If they are not in sync, neither organisational nor individual goals can be achieved. Hence assessment of organisation, individual, departmental needs must be assessed in order to improve the overall performance.

3. **Reviewing Documents:** Checking whether all the performance related documents are in place or not is the third important step that is followed in performance appraisal process. Inadequate documents might misguide during the process of performance goals setting. If this goes wrong, the organisations will not be able to achieve its goals of increased productivity and reduced attrition levels.

4. **Appropriate Setting:** Proper allocation of resources related to the performance goals must take place. If resources are not allocated properly they might not be of any help to the employees when needed. Hence appropriate setting of human as well as technical resources must take place.

5. **Deliver it Clearly:** Communication forms the basis of every single activity in the organisation. Whatever plan the organisation has in mind must be communicated to the employees in the most clear and transparent way. This helps the employees to relook at their performance and align it with the expectations of the organisation. Hence performance managing plan must be delivered to the employees clearly.

6. **Encourage:** The last point in the performance appraisal process is the encouragement of employees. They must be encouraged to follow the process and accomplish the targets that are set for them. When the employees are happy and encouraged they can be more productive on the job and as result monotony, work pressure, attrition etc. are easily avoided.

2.4.3 Types of Performance Appraisal

Performance appraisal is a very important process in the organisation. The significance and objectives of this process has been already discussed in the earlier paragraphs. Now we will focus on the various types / methods of conducting performance appraisal in the organisation. There are two major methods of performance appraisal viz., traditional methods and modern methods of performance appraisal. Let us look at each of the method in detail.

Traditional Methods of Performance Appraisal
1. **Rating Scales Method:** Rating scales is the most common method of performance appraisal. A rating form is composed of a number of scales, relating to certain job related dimensions including job knowledge, quality of work etc. Each rating contains a rating scale ranging from low to high wherein the supervisors have to rate their employees against the points stated. The rating scales are very well structured and standard. Rating scales provide a basis to the supervisor to compare and contrast the performance of the employees and select a rating scale.
2. **Essay Appraisal Method:** The essay method involves a supervisor's written report assessing an employee's performance, usually in terms of behaviour and output. The subject of essay method of appraisal is assessing the job performance of the employees in a detailed manner and it helps is deciding the appropriate rewards for the employees. Essay method of performance management is unstructured and hence can become unmanageable at times. This may lead to insufficient information and scope for a lot of biases.
3. **Ranking Method:** Ranking method involves comparison of employees against a job position that they are holding. It is often related to overall assessment of employee's performance rather than focusing on a single job component. Straight ranking needs the supervisor to rank a group of employees from best to bad considering the overall components. In case of limited employees and limited promotions, the ranking method can be really beneficial for differentiating the employees.
4. **Paired Comparison:** Paired comparison is a better method of performance management than the ranking method. In paired comparison the performance of individual employee is compared with each on in the team separately. After all the comparisons on the basis of overall results, the final rankings are given to the employees.
5. **Critical Incident Method:** The critical incident method of performance appraisal takes into consideration the description of each event about the employees where they have done exceptionally well or something that needs an improvement badly. This technique is totally dependent upon how the event was described and does not take into consideration any further rating or ranking scale. Critical incidents are stored in a very detailed manner and hence they can help the employees to improve their performance.
6. **Confidential Report System:** This method is mostly used in government organisations. This is a detailed and descriptive report prepared at the end of the year by the immediate supervisor of the employee. This report includes the description of strengths and weaknesses that the employee possesses. The

impression of the employee perceived by the supervisor is recorded in the confidential report. It does not include the mechanism of providing feedback to the appraisee as to how they are performing. Since these reports are confidential, they are not made open to the public especially the employees. Hence the employees never understand why they have got fewer grades than their colleagues and what area they need to improve in order to get better grades next time. Thus, there is very little scope in this method for performance improvement.

7. **Checklist Method:** Checklist is the simplest type of individual performance assessment technique. A checklist includes a list of statements containing the behaviour and traits of the employees. If the supervisor thinks that a particular behaviour and a particular trait is suitable to an employee he checks them all. Similarly it is done for all the remaining statements in the checklist.

8. **Forced Distribution:** This is a rating scale where the supervisors are required to rate an employee on the basis of specific choices given to them.

Modern Methods of Performance Appraisal

1. **Assessment Centres:** An assessment centre is a location where managers from all the departments across the organisation can come together and get their output measured from trained observers. This method at first was used by the Gernamn Army in 1930 and then by the British army in 1960. This method typically evaluates the current performance of the employee and at the same time focuses on identifying his potential for performing other jobs in the future. Techniques like management games, role plays, in-basket training exercise are used in assessment centres. Also other methods such as personal interview, written tests etc. are used to evaluate an employee's intellectual capacities required for the job.

2. **Behaviourally Anchored Rating Scales:** This method includes graphic rating scale and critical incident method together. Under this method, the top management sets the behaviour determinants of a particular position and these are considered as standards. The performance behaviour of the employees is then compared against the predetermined behaviour pattern and accordingly grades are given to them.

3. **Human Resource Accounting:** Human resources are the most important and valuable assets in the organisation and it is possible to value them in monetary terms. This method evaluates the performance of the employee in cost and return terms. HR costs include money spent on recruitment, selection, manpower planning, training, development etc. The performance of the employee is evaluated on the basis of the amount of money spent on him and the contributions he has made against the

money spent. Human Resource Accounting method is still under development and hence not very popular in the organisations.

4. **Management by Objectives:** Management By Objectives popularly known as MBO is a very effective and modern method of performance appraisal. This is regarded as the most systematic and result oriented method of all, with very less scope for biases or prejudices. This concept was introduced by Peter Drucker in 1954. This method basically talks about the goal setting approach in performance management. In this method, the supervisor/manager and the employee sit together and set goals for the success of the organisation and decide the responsibilities to be shared by each individual in order to accomplish the set objectives.

2.4.4 Achieving Effective Performance Appraisal

Performance appraisal is an activity for which managers and employees are equally responsible. And hence making the process more effective is the priority of the employees and management. Given below are a few points that help achieving effective performance appraisal in the organisation.

1. **Explain the Appraisal Process:** To make the appraisal process effective it must be ensured that everyone included in the process has understood the process very well. If the objectives, components and outcomes are not clear to the employees or to the management, the purpose of performance appraisal will not be achieved. Hence explaining the process to everyone is the most important part of implementing the appraisal system in the organisation.

2. **Clarify Job Expectations:** Mutual understanding of job expectations must be done before the performance appraisal happens in the organisation. Employees must know the standards against which their performance is going to be evaluated in terms of skills, job knowledge, productivity, output etc.

3. **Review and Update Job Skills:** Performance appraisal is a continuous process in the organisation. Hence one process must give rise to setting goals for the next appraisal period. For this, the performance of the employees must be consciously checked, reviewed and due feedback must be shared with the employees, which helps the employees to update themselves in order to meet the set goals and they must be given sufficient time for upgrading their skills, knowledge and attitudes.

4. **Rewards Management:** Performance appraisal means appraising, recognising the performance given by employees in a specific period of time. It has been observed that rewards always motivate an individual to perform better. And hence when the performance goals are supported by rewards, employees tend to be more serious about goals achievement and overall objective of the organisation can be achieved easily.

2.5 Monitoring and Mentoring

2.5.1 Introduction

Monitoring and mentoring are both very essential processes in an organisation for overall improvement in the performance management process. Usually management at the top, plans for performance management system in the organisation and the employees working under them are required to execute the plan. When monitoring happens, the problems and grey areas in the implementation of the performance management system can be easily identified, and remedial measures can be adopted immediately. This saves future losses of, time, money and productivity.

2.5.2 Importance of Monitoring

Given below are the benefits of monitoring process:

1. **Prevents Business Disruption:** Constant monitoring helps to identify the defects in the performance at an early stage and remedial measures can be taken up immediately. Hence early identification of errors and problems in the performance improvement programme helps the mentor to identify future course of action and business disruptions can be prevented successfully. As monitoring is always followed by providing timely feedback, this also ensures good quality of service and timely service.

2. **Rapid and Successful Development of New Technologies:** Since monitoring happens on a regular basis, the management understands the capabilities of the employees for undertaking challenges. Once the strengths and weaknesses of the employees are identified, it becomes easy for the organisation to plan for the acquisition and installment of latest technology for rapid development of the organisation.

3. **Increase Customer Acquisition and Retention:** Quality is the basis of every activity that is conducted in the organisation. Hence if the customers are happy they will bring in more customers who would like to stay on for a longer period of time. Also by monitoring the progress of employees, it becomes simple for the management to make the employees quality conscious and this in turn helps the organisation in attracting new customers and retain customer base as long as possible.

2.5.3 Role of Mentor in the Organisation

Mentoring is another effective tool that monitors the performance of the employees in a more informal way. A mentor is just like a friend of the employee and guides him in every aspect of his life, be it personal or professional. The main focus of mentoring is overall development of the employee and helping the employee strike a balance between personal life and professional life. Hence by striking the balance, the employee becomes more productive at work. This increases the profitability of the organisation and creates a win-win situation. A mentor is the most influential person and regarded as the most knowledgeable in the organisation. He is responsible for the upward mobility of the human resources in the organisation. Given below are six ways that explain the role of a mentor in the organisation.

1. **Develop and Manage Mentoring Relationship:** A mentor in the organisation is responsible for developing and maintaining mentor mentee relationships in the organisation. It begins with assessing the readiness and ability of the mentor himself to take up the activity of developing others. This mentoring relationship thus takes a form of building trust, setting goals and keeping this mentoring relationship on track.

2. **Create Opportunities to Socialise:** The mentor must provide opportunities to the mentee to become more social and make his/her strengths visible to all the other employees in the organisation. This activity helps to build confidence in the minds of the employees and they start trusting the intentions of their mentor. This is very important in a mentor – mentee relationship.

3. **Survey the Environment:** A mentor is responsible for every decision he takes for his mentees, as the success and failure of the mentee's career solely depends upon the direction given by their mentor. To achieve the perfect decision making skills, the mentor must scan and understand the environment around him. Conducting SWOT analysis of the environment always benefits the mentor in holistic decision making.

4. **Guide and Counsel:** As mentioned earlier, the mentor is just like a friend, philosopher and guide of the mentees assigned to him. He needs to provide them guidance for every step they wish to take or every career path they want to lead. Similarly when employees are disturbed with certain issues or not able to be productive on the job, the mentor is supposed to counsel them and bring them back on to their normal track.

5. **Be a Role Model:** A mentor must set an example for other employees and be their role model. Because just by observing, employees can learn many things such as honesty, integrity, ethics, values etc. if the mentor himself has all these in his behaviour, the same can be adopted by the mentees working under him.

6. **Motivate and Inspire:** A mentor's support always encourages their mentees. When they receive support from their mentor regarding setting goals, improving performance, achieving targets etc. the employees become more motivated and encouraged to work better at the job.

2.5.4 Supervision

Supervision is an integral part of monitoring. Supervision is a more formal form of monitoring where each and every activity of the employees is closely monitored, like what they are doing, how they are doing etc.

The task of supervision within the workplace often proves challenging as supervisors are commonly tasked with monitoring a large number of employees at one time. This proves particularly true within the realm of small business, where the number of managerial employees may be limited. While overseeing a large group of employees is decidedly more difficult than monitoring just one or two workers, it is a task that can be mastered if you employ some useful strategies.

The biggest challenge in supervising a large number of employees at once is often keeping track of information about each worker. To simplify this task, create chronological supervision files for each worker in your charge. When taking notes about employees, completing employee reviews or reviewing employee work, note the date at the top of each new piece of documentation. When placing these pieces of documentation in files, organise them by these dates, ensuring that they can be reviewed easily, giving you a clear picture of the employee's timeline as a worker within the company.

2.5.5 Objectives of Monitoring Performance

The objectives of monitoring performance are as follows:

1. Evaluating the effectiveness of the implemented measures and determining whether additional measures are required;
2. Monitoring the improvement of the native vegetation / fauna habitat within the Project Area over time; and
3. Assessing progress towards meeting the success criteria.

2.5.6 Principles of Monitoring

1. Do a Performance Improvement Analysis

First, measure the frequency of behaviour (what the individual says or the physical movements made) and the outputs (the physical evidence of completed work produced by those behaviours) prior to any management change. This analysis can be done for just one behaviour and output or for many by job category, department and organisation. Through this analysis, one measures present performance, establishes standards, specifies why behaviour is deficient, calculates the net economic value of improvement after the cost of solutions, and places them in priority order. The result of this analysis is identification of potentially high-payoff behaviours and outputs that can be improved - an important first step, because, surprisingly, key behaviours and outputs are often overlooked or undervalued in organisations.

The next step is to introduce the procedures used in Performance Management and quantify the amount of change that occurs in specific time periods. Because the investment in changing behaviour is often very low and the economic payoffs may be high, the potential high return on investment usually excites top management.

2. Be Specific

Describe and communicate desired performances and the standards for judging them in terms that are measurable, observable and objective. A description of the events that are signals prompting the response should be included. In training, coaching, measuring performance, feeding back performance data, conducting a performance appraisal, writing procedures, and delivering positive reinforcement, it is essential to be specific. Unfortunately, if the language used is vague, the desired behaviour may not occur.

3. Measure

For any performance shown by the analysis to have sufficient economic value to an organisation, measure the frequency of the performance against the desired standards. While most organisations measure some performance, there are, unfortunately, many key outputs and behaviours that are not measured.

4. Give Feedback

Provide feedback on performance to the individual involved and to the individual's manager, supervisor, or group leader, rapidly-preferably immediately-with sufficient information to allow for self-correction. Too often, feedback systems for many key behaviours and outputs are either absent or flawed.

5. Deliver Positive Consequences

Deliver to each individual positive consequences immediately after completion of the performance of the desired behaviours and outputs. The frequency of an individual's behaviour is affected by the consequences that follow it. If the consequences are positive to that individual, the behaviour tends to increase; if they are negative, the behaviour tends to decrease. Consequences should be delivered for as long as the performance is desired, or until naturally occurring consequences are strong enough to support the behaviour. How frequently you provide positive consequences is determined by how often the behaviour occurs, the phase of behaviour change you are in (causing the first new behaviour to occur, changing its frequency, or maintaining it) and the pattern of responses you desire (steady, maximum output, peak for certain periods, etc.)

Unfortunately, in many organisations the wrong consequence system is in place. Consequences of desired behaviour are often negative or neutral. Undesired behaviour may be rewarded. The reinforcers are badly delayed. They are delivered only on a group basis (annual company-wide profit sharing). The rewards are short-lived for behaviour that is desired long-term. And almost always the positive reinforcement is too infrequent.

2.5.7 Monitoring Process

1. **Conducting a Readiness Assessment:** Before implementing the monitoring process in the organisation, it must be ensured that the employees working in the organisation are

ready for it, because the success of any new system depends upon how the employees perceive it. And hence to check whether employees are ready to accept the monitoring process or not, the readiness assessment is conducted.

2. **Agreeing on Outcomes to Monitor and Evaluate:** Once the readiness of the employees is ascertained regarding the process of monitoring, the outcomes to be achieved are decided. This happens mutually. This way, the employees understand what they need to achieve in the particular time period and management understands what they need to monitor during that particular time period.

3. **Selecting Key Indicators to Monitor Outcomes:** This includes the scale that will be used for assessing the performance, the points at which observations will be made, and the frequency with which the outcomes will be measured and recorded.

4. **Baseline Data on each Indicator:** This includes writing a brief description about each performance indicator. Like what you want to achieve, where are you today, where you want to go? This is still in the planning phase.

5. **Planning for Improvement:** During this stage the results targets are selected, so that it becomes easier during monitoring the performance of the employees as to what outcomes to expect and how to measure them against the standards.

6. **Monitoring for Results:** Results must be made the focus of prime importance while planning for implementing the monitoring process in the organisation. When the process becomes results specific, the system becomes more concrete and concise.

7. **Write a Rough Draft of the Monitoring and Evaluation System:** Once the plan is ready, the responsible persons need to share the same with the experienced people in the organisation. This helps to identify loopholes if any, in the process and can be eliminated beforehand so that the process is flawless. Make the necessary changes and make the document out for public reference.

2.6 Periodic Reviews

Performance management is an ongoing process in organisations. In order to make the organisation successful and progressing, it is very important to have it going in the organisation continuously. And when this happens regularly it comes in the form of periodic reviews.

Through constant research it has been identified that employees need feedback on the performance that they have shown. Some sort of encouragement and motivation is required while on the job. Feedback shared by the management may be positive or negative, helps employees to enhance their performance and be a better person on the job.

Another point why employees need feedback is many a times, the performance appraisal system is reward based, i.e. the performance of the employee when evaluated gets appropriate rewards to enhance the motivational level of the employees. Hence to get rewards and earn status for themselves employees seek feedback from the management.

Now, it is the responsibility of the management to share periodic reviews with the employees on how they are performing and where they need to improve in order to be eligible for rewards or to be able to contribute to the overall objective achievement of the organisation.

Periodic reviews simply mean, assessing the performance of the employees regularly after a specific time interval. Employees are given certain short term goals to achieve and their performance is evaluated on the basis of this goal achievement. This helps the employees gain confidence and understand the bigger picture much clearly.

2.7 Problem Solving in Performance Management

The performance of the employee in the organisation is dependent upon many factors including his potential, technical know-how, knowledge of the organisation, competencies etc. It is the integration of all the skills of the employees that make him the best performer in the organisation. Unless the employee has sufficient amount of knowledge, skills and attitudes, he/she cannot be effective on the job. If the job that is allotted to the employee is not giving him the opportunity to solve problems and use his knowledge, skills and attitude, he is likely to be frustrated at the job and his motivation level is likely to be low.

Problem solving is a highly-cognitive process that needs the person to know how to deal with a problem and get to the solution in the most appropriate manner. Problem solving is the most crucial skill required to be possessed by the managers and leaders. The occurrence of problem solving phase comes at the time of evaluation and review phase of performance appraisal.

Problem solving is undertaken with a specific objective, for example, ascertaining why an employee is unable to achieve desired level of performance in spite of getting all the other things right. This requires high level of skills possessed by the managers who are assessing the performance of the employees.

Problem solving also involves the process of decision making and hence is the problem is solved completely and effectively, and then the decision making can happen in the most effective manner. Appropriate solution can be provided to the employees in order to improving their performance if the detection of problem has happened accurately.

Following are the points to be remembered during problem solving

1. Use creative strategies for problem solving
2. Try and generate outstanding solutions to the problem
3. Focus on solving the problems rather than indicators

4. Use logical and analytical skills
5. Approach problem with open mind away from biases
6. Don't be afraid to make mistakes

2.8 Engendering Trust in Performance Management

Performance management is a relatively new concept in the field of management. Performance management includes the integration of skills, knowledge, attitudes and mutual trust that the employees and the management has on the process.

Trust is the bond between an organisation and employees. We know that it is very difficult to be in a relationship with someone or work with someone whom we don't trust. In order to get the most out of employees and make them achieve the organisational goals and objectives, it is very important that you trust them and they trust you in return. Given below are few points for engendering trust in the organisation.

1. Be open and communicate important issues to the employees. The more the process is transparent, the more employees will trust the process and the organisation,
2. Always provide such assignments to the employees that will make them stretch their abilities. This will make them understand that the process is for the development of their personal career.
3. Actively listening to what the employees are saying and being open to their needs always help in stimulating the trust of the employees.
4. Always being ethical in approach helps the management to gain trust very easily from the employees.
5. Involving employees in decision making and meetings.
6. Being respectful while talking to people working in the organisation.
7. Supporting and encouraging employees in whatever they do.
8. Maintaining confidentiality wherever required.

2.9 Role Efficacy

Role efficacy would mean potential effectiveness of an individual occupying a particular role in an organisation. **Role efficacy** is the potential effectiveness of a role.

Dimensions of Role Efficacy :

1. **Centrality Vs. Pripherality :** The dimension of centrality measures the role occupants' perception of the significance of the role. The more central that a manager feels his her role is in the organisation, the higher will be his her role efficacy.

2. **Integration Vs. Distance :** Integration between the self and the role contributes to role efficacy and self-role distance diminishes efficacy.
3. **Proactivity Vs. Reactivity :** When a role occupant takes some initiative and does something independently, that person is exhibiting proactive behaviour. On the other hand, if she merely responds to what others expect, the behaviour is reactive.
4. **Creativity Vs. Routinism :** When a role occupant perceives that they do something new or unique in their roles, their efficacy is high. The perception that they do only routine tasks lowers role efficacy.
5. **Linkage Vs. Isolation :** Inter-role linkage contributes to role efficacy. If role occupants perceive interdependence with others, their efficacy will be high. Isolation of roles reduces efficacy.
6. **Helping vs. Hostility :** One important aspect of efficacy is the individual's perception of how he/she gives or receives help. A perception of hostility decreases efficacy.
7. **Super-ordination Vs. Deprivation :** One dimension of role efficacy is the perception that the role occupants contribute to some larger entity.
8. **Influence Vs. Powerlessness :** The role occupants' feeling that they are able to exercise influence in their roles increases their efficacy. The influence may be in terms of decision-making, implementation, advice or problem solving.
9. **Growh Vs. Stagnation :** When a role occupant has opportunities and perceives them as such - to develop in his/her role through learning new things, role efficacy is likely to be high. Similarly, if the individual perceives his/her role as lacking in opportunities for growth, the role efficacy will be low.
10. **Conformation Vs. Avoidance :** When problems arise, they can either be confronted to find solutions or they can be avoided. Confronting problems to find solutions contributes to efficacy and avoidance reduces efficacy.

Points to Remember

- Components of Manager's Performance and Development Plans
    1. Ascertaining Performance Development Needs
    2. Appraisal of Present Management Talent
    3. Planning of Individual Development Program
    4. Competency based Performance Training
- Objectives of Performance Managing
    1. Increase Two Way Communication
    2. Identify and Resolve Performance Problems

3. Recognize Quality Performance
4. Providing data for administrative purposes
- Process of Performance Managing
    1. Planning
    2. Monitoring
    3. Developing
    4. Rating
    5. Rewarding
- Importance of Performance Management
    1. Involving Employee in the Planning Stage
    2. Monitoring the Progress of the Employees
    3. Ensuring All Round Development of the Employees
    4. Evaluation of Individual Performance
- Performance appraisal is a systematic evaluation of an individual's performance with respect to actual performance of the job and standard performance expected by the organisation.
- Performance Appraisal Process
    1. Preparation
    2. Assessment
    3. Reviewing Documents
    4. Appropriate Setting
    5. Deliver it Clearly
    6. Encourage
- Traditional Methods of Performance Appraisal
    1. Rating Scales Method
    2. Essay Appraisal Method
    3. Ranking Method
    4. Paired Comparison
    5. Critical Incident Method
    6. Confidential Report System
    7. Checklist Method
    8. Forced Distribution
- Modern Methods of Performance Appraisal
    1. Assessment Centres

2. Behaviourally Anchored Rating Scales
3. Human Resource Accounting
4. Management by Objective

Questions for Discussion

1. What are the organisational and individual performance plans and components of a manager's development plan? Why are setting mutual expectations and performance criteria important?
2. Explain the objectives, process and importance of performance managing.
3. Explain the objectives, process of performance appraisal types and guidelines for achieving effective performance appraisal.
4. Discuss the objectives, principles and process of Monitoring.
5. Write short notes on:
   (a) Periodic reviews
   (b) Problem solving
   (c) Engendering trust and
   (d) Role efficacy relating to performance management

Project Questions

1. How would you set goals for your subordinates? Do you think this would help in managing performance of your subordinate?
2. Prepare an appraisal form for a sales executive. Describe what approach for evaluation has been used and why? Indicate whether the appraisal would be confidential or open and why? How do you think the form suggested would help individual development?

Chapter **3**...

Implementing Performance Management

Contents ...

3.1 Implementing Performance Management
    3.1.1 Introduction
    3.1.2 Pre-requisites for Performance Management System
    3.1.3 Actions Required for Performance Management System
    3.1.4 Process of Implementing Performance Management
    3.1.5 Tips to Successfully Implement Performance Management
    3.1.6 Keys to a Successful Performance Management System
    3.1.7 Challenges in Implementing Performance Management

3.2 Strategies for Effective Implementation of Performance Management

3.3 Reasons for the Use of Advanced Performance Management Techniques

3.4 Top Management Agreement, Commitment and Leadership
    3.4.1 Role of Top Managers in Performance Management
    3.4.2 Role of Line Managers in Performance Management

3.5 Building Performance Oriented Work Culture

3.6 Factors Affecting the Effective Use of Performance Management
    3.6.1 Design
    3.6.2 Training
    3.6.3 Employee Development
    3.6.4 Corporate Culture
    3.6.5 Review and Update

- Points to Remember
- Questions for Discussion
- Project Questions

Learning Objectives ...
- To have a basic understanding of implementation of Performance Management System
- To be able to explain the strategies involved in effective implementation of performance management system
- To discuss top management agreement, commitment and leadership in Performance Management System
- To explain the factors in building performance oriented work culture
- To understand the factors affecting use of performance management

3.1 Implementing Performance Management

3.1.1 Introduction

The role of HR in the dynamic world of today has undergone multiple changes. Its main focus is on improving the performance of the employees by evolving functional strategies. HR always works towards facilitating and improving the performance of the employees in order to meet the corporate and strategic goals. Today, all the strategies of HR are directed towards producing high performing work systems and high performing leaders.

Performance management is the latest trend now and is the need of the hour. If the performance of the employees is not managed in an effective way, the organisation will not be able to achieve its objectives of profit maximization and growth. The process of performance management begins when an employee joins the organisation and ends when he/she quits the organisation. However, in between his/her journey with the organisation, there needs to be a systematic operation of the performance management process.

3.1.2 Pre-requisites for Performance Management System

Some of the essential pre-requisites without which performance management system will not function effectively in an organisation are :

- The performance management process cannot function on its own. It needs the support of all the employees. Hence, high level of participation is required in order to generate an effective performance management system.
- No process in the organisation can be implemented without the support of top management. Thus top management's help and assistance must be requested for the smooth implementation and functioning of the process.

- Before implementing the performance management system, it must be confirmed that all the employees have clearly understood the vision and mission statements of the organisation. This is because when the vision and mission is clear to the employees, their performance can be directed towards achievement of the same.
- Role clarity and the relationship of the particular role with other roles must be clear to the employees. This improves the performance in terms of team effort, group building etc. And when employees understand the relationship of their role with other roles, they tend perform better.
- Along with improving the processes, communication across the departments in the organisation must be clear and transparent. Open channels of communication builds trust among the employees and they feel valued. When the trust in the minds of employees is built, they tend to perform on the guidelines given by the organisation.
- Identification of performance parameters and key performance indicators must be done and shared with the employees to generate the standard level of performance from them.
- There must be a high level of transparency, consistency and openness in the applied processes.
- The performance management system must be complimented with better rewards and recognition policy. Performance can be improved if employees know what are the rewards associated with it.
- Performance management system must also have provision for proper training. Training must be provided to supervisors and employees, for better review of their performance and further improvement and corrections, if any.

3.1.3 Actions Required for Performance Management System

According to Armstrong and Baron (1998), Performance Management is both a strategic and integrated approach to achieve successful results in the organisation. This can happen through improving the capabilities of individuals and teams. Performance management system includes the following actions.

- Developing clear job descriptions and performance plan indicators in order to set Key Result Areas (KRAs) for the employees.
- Selecting the right kind of people for implementing and executing the process of performance management system.
- Analysing the performance and outcomes achieved as regards the performance standards set.

- Providing continuous, constructive and regular feedback for consistently improving the performance of the employees.
- Constant support for career development and guidance for meeting individual current and future goals.
- Designing encouraging reward system in line with the performance standards.

3.1.4 Process of Implementing Performance Management

1. Clarify Objectives

A vital first step is identifying some major objectives for the program. Clarifying the need for a performance management system, what and who it should include, what it will deliver and agreeing measures of what a successful implementation will look like.

Some organisations choose to complete this step collaboratively with inputs from various employee groups; others delegate this as an HR Department responsibility; some organisations have a particular champion from anywhere within the business; others will involve outside consultants. Any of these methodologies can work.

Whoever is involved in clarifying the objective, a good start is to use the definition above: improving performance and satisfaction.

It is also vital to consider the business benefits rather than presenting the concept only from an employee's perspective.

Many systems fail because they try to do too much and become too complex. Once a system is running effectively and delivering the expected results, it may be possible to add additional objectives when all parties have confidence in it and can see the value.

Experience suggests that a business needs to complete a self examination before committing to implementing a new performance management system:

(a) Do employees believe the work we do here is "worthwhile" and that their individual jobs make a contribution to this?

(b) Do we have clear organisational values which we demonstrate consistently? Do we "walk the talk"?

(c) Are employees confident that if they do the right thing they will be recognised for that and appropriately rewarded?

(d) If the organisation cannot confidently answer in the positive in each of the three areas, then it helps to be aware of where there may be shortfalls and seek to address such issues concurrently with implementing the performance management system to increase its chances of success.

(e) A clear and communicated company vision, supported by clarity in people's jobs helps deliver the first element;
(f) Documented, communicated and demonstrated core competencies helps with the second;
(g) Formal and informal rewards which are seen as transparent, consistent and fair will help deliver the third.

2. Secure Senior Manager Buy-in

Once the objectives are set with associated expected business outcomes, then the agreement of the senior management team is required before any implementation steps are taken.

Most systems fail because they are seen as outside a manager's day-to-day responsibilities, rather than integral to them – senior managers must believe in the process and be seen to actively support it, "talking it up" at every opportunity and leading by example with line managers who report to them.

It is important for senior managers to have a realistic understanding of how much management time will be required to implement and then integrate this system on an ongoing basis.

(a) Experience tells us that more time is required in the first year and, conversely, the first year usually delivers the poorest results.
(b) Understanding of the system, how it works and what it will deliver; and developing the skills necessary to carry our effective performance management often take time – more time than expected.
(c) Having a clear understanding of the potential benefits is vital to securing the necessary support of senior managers.

3. Prepare the System and Supporting Materials and Documentation

Develop a process and documentation to support the system.

The format of the documentation is less important than the prompts included for managers and their staff to confidently address the key areas. The minimum prompts must include opportunity to:

(a) Review performance against the key parts of the job.
(b) Review performance against any specific goals or objectives which have been set.
(c) Review performance against the organisation's core competencies if they have been defined.
(d) Identify any learning and development needs for both short and longer term.

(e) Set goals for the next period.

(f) Allow for feedback on progress on an ongoing basis.

Ensure job descriptions are current and in a form that provide clear and measurable results.

If they are to be used, ensure core competencies are defined with associated behaviours and are communicated to all staff.

Determine how direct the link will be with pay review – will there be an overall rating system or not?

(a) The main advantage of a direct link is enhanced objectivity in the pay review process.

(b) The main disadvantage is a risk that the rating may become disproportionately important during the process and focus is lost on the other objectives of the performance management and development program.

Make the documentation easy to use – providing hard copy or electronic or web-based.

Consider the system as a cycle with goal setting, progress reviews and recognition/feedback on achievement and then determine a calendar for the key elements of the cycle. For example:

(a) Will goal setting be completed annually or six monthly?

(b) Will progress reviews be every month or two months?

(c) Will the formal achievement review – the formal performance management and development interview – be annually or six months and how will it fit with the pay review timetable and the annual business plans?

The timing of the calendar should meet your organisation's specific needs. Experience tells us that more frequent progress reviews save time in the long run and help the process deliver better results.

4. **Ensure Managers are Trained**

When the process is agreed and supporting documentation in place, training is the next key step. Most performance management systems fail because of lack of training of the people involved.

Managers should be trained in the following:

(a) The objective of the system.

(b) The benefits of effective performance management – for them, for the business and for their staff.

(c) Their responsibility for the system.

(d) The particular process you are going to use – and why.

(e) Setting objectives – why and how
(f) Measuring results – do the hard work up front.
(g) Providing feedback – what and how.
(h) Addressing performance issues – why and how.
(i) Identifying development needs –why and how.

Managing performance is often an assumed skill – in practice many line managers find this difficult and welcome development in this area. The development should include a mix of soft skills and process management as suggested above and should focus on this being an integral element of the line manager's role – not an additional or administrative burden. Their own success will be impacted by how well they carry out this vital responsibility.

If a manager cannot articulate a simple and common reason for using the performance management and development process, and be supportive of it, then it is unlikely the programme will be a success.

A typical training workshop to achieve this may run for one and a half days for each small group to allow understanding and skills to develop to the required level. Experience suggests that refresher sessions should also be scheduled.

5. Ensure all Participant Employees are Trained

Most performance management systems fail because of lack of training of the people involved.

For the employee groups selected to be included in the programme, training should include the following:

(a) The objective of the system.
(b) The benefits of effective performance management – for them individually and for the business.
(c) Their responsibility within the system – linked to delivering the expected benefits.
(d) The particular process you are going to use – and why
(e) Preparation – what they need to do to make the most of the process.
(f) Setting objectives –why and how.
(g) Measuring results – doing the hard work up front.
(h) Identifying development needs and own aspirations.

Such training sessions can be completed with groups and each may run for a couple of hours or so – this can be included in the induction program for new staff after the initial launch of the programme.

6. Launch with Champion

A senior management champion for the process should be identified and should take responsibility for launching the programme in an appropriate forum, outlining the major objectives and expected benefits.

Subsequent to launching the programme, the champion should continually seek opportunities to explore how the programme is working, address opportunities to enhance it, "talk it up" and set the expectation that this is a core element of the organisation's business process.

7. Monitor and Review Success

A schedule should be set and followed for reviewing the implementation of the programme against key milestones and against the success measures which were determined in Step 1.

Most systems require some adjustment during the first couple of years – those which had clear objectives in the first place and were supported by appropriate training and senior management endorsement, are most likely to succeed.

It is quite usual for other employee management processes to be reviewed during this time also to ensure full integration of the materials, techniques and supporting mechanisms. We strongly recommend using our training workshop manuals for training both managers and employees in the process of performance management to ensure a greater chance of success.

3.1.5 Tips to Successfully Implement Performance Management

1. Ensure the [performance management] system is aligned with your organisation's management practices. Ensure that the system targets similar competencies as those that managers, owners, or HR use to recruit, staff, and train. Even though the person, people, or department doing the hiring for your organisation may not directly manage the organisation's performance management system, they are not mutually exclusive. Therefore, hiring managers should be consulted and involved in all aspects of the performance management processes.
2. Elicit the help and support of organisational members, aiming to get the support of top leaders and managers. Support from all parties involved will greatly increase the success of a performance management system. A large hurdle in implementing a system will be gaining support. Some staff may feel threatened by the prospect of being evaluated on

their performance and that performance will be linked to pay and promotion. The notion can provoke emotional negative responses and cause some opposition and undermining of the system. The support attained from leaders and managers will help to bypass some of these issues. Open communication with all affected parties is important; inform and consult with them throughout the process of establishing the performance management system.

3. Get the CEO to demonstrate their support for the system. While eliciting support is crucial, they must also communicate their support. The CEO and top management need to be vocal about their support for performance management. Create email messages, videos, and briefings that discuss the importance of the system and educate on the value of performance management. Use surveys to check on employees' satisfaction with management's role in the performance management process and use these to address any issues.

4. Automate the performance management system using a technology-based approach to maintain and update records. There are many software programmes designed for performance management and the benefits are numerous: data analysis, information sharing, and greater efficiency in maintaining performance records. Performance management technology can help save time and reduce the effort needed to manage the system. Train both employees and managers on how to use the performance management system.

5. Pilot test on a group of employees and managers to identify any issues before applying it to the whole organisation. A pilot test will help iron out any small problems and you can assess the greater impact upon employees. It will be especially helpful for organisations without prior performance management training or experience. Evaluate and improve the process.

6. Decide on the primary purpose of the performance management system: will it be for decision-making or development? Choose one and then create a system that will support this purpose. Having a defined purpose will help the system achieve the best possible results. A system that tries to incorporate both purposes will ultimately be letting itself down, since both cannot be given due focus. If your system's primary purpose is both, then try to treat each purpose separately and conduct separate discussions for decision-making and development.

7. Managers play a key role in performance management and they need to embrace this role. They are responsible for ensuring that employees have the training and skills they

need. They are also responsible for assessing performance. They must demonstrate courage by providing frequent and accurate feedback to employees. In reality, there is often a disconnect between managers and performance management. Most managers understand what they need to be doing, yet they don't actually go through with doing it. Encourage managers to embrace their roles by highlighting the importance of performance management to both the organisation and the employees.

8. Hire managers with competencies that equip them to successfully implement performance management. As managers play such a key role, those with the right competencies and experiences are ideal and they can enhance performance management. Communication skills, sound judgment, and fairness are examples of these competencies. Managers that tend to give positive feedback and can provide rewards to high performing employees.

9. Top leaders develop performance management policies. The responsibility for designing effective performance management policies is with the very top management. They will need to define and take action upon the organisation's core values of performance. Top management will set the tone for the line managers in whom they will motivate to see the instrumental value of performance management for the organisation. Top leaders and managers need to be held accountable for fully implementing the performance management system.

10. Finally, stick to your performance management system like glue. If your commitment to the system diminishes, so will the effectiveness of your system. Keep in check that you will faithfully and fully support the system right through the entire process. You don't want all the hard work you put into implementing a performance management system to go to disuse and waste. Keep your sight on the benefits that this will bring: increased performance, increased employee motivation, and achieving the organisation's goals and visions for the future.

3.1.6 Keys to a Successful Performance Management System

Before you develop your action plan in detail, let's look at five keys things, in addition to culture, which serve as a foundation for a successful performance management system:

1. **Communicate Expectations:** People want to know what is expected of them. A great way to start is to verify that job descriptions are accurate and to help your employees establish S.M.A.R.T. goals. As you interact with your employees on a regular basis, use the

goals as a tool to keep employees focused on the expectations. Keep in mind that your ultimate goal is for employees to take responsibility for their own performance. They are more likely to do this when they work with you in partnership to clarify performance expectations.

2. **Involve Employees in the Process:** Employees always want to know the answer to the question, WIIFM, or what's in it for me? Your employees' commitment to performance management will depend on how they perceive the answer to that question. In order to have a true partnership, you have to involve your employees at each step in the performance management process: planning, monitoring, analysing, improving, and maintaining. When you involve your employees in the process you are on your way to establishing performance management as a win-win system.

3. **Use a Systematic Approach:** Performance management is not just setting goals. It's not just doing annual performance appraisals. It's not providing occasional performance feedback. Performance management is a system that encompasses all of these things and much more. The system works best when managers and employees are actively engaged in each step in the process. Then, the whole becomes greater than the sum of the individual steps.

4. **Be Willing to Work Hard:** Implementing performance management takes time and effort. There will need to be lots of one-on-one meetings with employees as well as some team meetings. You and your employees may even experience "brain strain" if you are setting goals and objectives for the first time. As you and your employees become more experienced, however, the process should require less time up front so that more time can be spent in doing the work required to achieve the goals. Performance management is a partnership. You don't do the work for your employees. They have to work hard too, if the system is going to work.

5. **Make a Commitment to Success:** Are you really committed to implementing performance management? If not, then success will be limited or even nonexistent. You have to take the lead in communicating your commitment to your employees. They will know whether your commitment is total or half-hearted. In the end, their commitment will be a reflection of your commitment. Your commitment must be maintained throughout the process. If you don't conduct a performance review on time, you are delivering a message about your level of commitment. If you don't follow up on established goals, employees will take this as a sign that you lack commitment to the goals. If performance management is to have long term success, you have to have long-term goals.

3.1.7 Challenges in Implementing Performance Management

The performance management challenge in organisations has many dimensions in today's business environment and creating focused initiatives to overcome these challenges is not a silver bullet approach. In many cases remuneration schemes are driving the performance system, which creates a number on long term consequences in organisational behaviour and culture. In other cases senior management are so focused on scorecard management to hold people accountable that the creation of the scorecard is not aligned with business focus areas, but rather a number of deliverable projects and tasks.

1. **Lack of Alignment:** The first challenge is the lack of alignment due to various organisational processes being created in isolation. The link between strategy development, budgeting and operational planning is developed by different groups of people with different frameworks being used. The performance management system lacks alignment between individual performance, departmental performance and organisational delivery and so all systems default back to financial measurements.

2. **Lack of Measurements:** The second challenge happens at various levels of the organisation in that poor measures are developed, in many cases targets are set but no relevant measure is put in place. In other cases no data can be collected or is kept as evidence to track performance.

3. **Leadership and Management Commitment:** The Leadership and Management challenge has a huge impact on integrating and aligning a management system to deliver a comprehensive performance management system. The commitment and understanding of leadership and management of the requirements for achieving a workable performance system is critical to performance success.

4. **Managing of the Performance System:** Managing a performance system in an organisation requires a disciplined framework; it requires the organisation to work off one master plan broken down into relevant parts and areas of responsibility. The management responsibility at various levels needs to understand the contracting, measurement development and appraisal process very well and apply it consistently. Secondly, management needs to appreciate that performance management is not an event but something that is managed daily but recorded and reported at certain times through reviews and appraisals.

5. **Managing Poor Performances:** The management of poor performance is normally a reactive action, but in many cases, it is delayed and therefore turns into a discussion that is difficult to make relevant. Another reason why poor performance is not managed on time is the lack of valid measurements and the collection of required evidence and measurement data.

3.2 Strategies for Effective Implementation of Performance Management

Performance management is a very critical process in the organisation. And hence it must be implemented very carefully in the organisation. As every step taken under performance management process is only for the performance enhancement of the employees. If the performance of the employees is not developed in a proper manner, then it would be impossible for the organisation to meet its strategic and organisational goals.

The steps given below are the strategies adopted by organisations these days for effective implementation of performance management strategies.

1. **Define the Need:** While implementing any type of performance management program in the organisation, it must be noted that, the need identification must happen properly. If the need is not identified properly, the performance improvement efforts will not reach the strategic aims and objectives of the organisation. Hence need assessment as to why performance must be managed needs to be ascertained in the beginning.

2. **Determining Strategy:** Once the needs are assessed, a strategy must be identified as to how the organisation is going to move further and how the needs are to be met through performance management efforts.

3. **Aligning Business Strategy with Performance Management Strategy:** This is the most critical part of strategy while implementing performance management process in the organisation. The goals and objectives of the performance management initiative must match with those of organisation to create a win-win situation.

4. **Selection of Resources:** To successfully implement performance management process in the organisation, competent people are required. Hence it becomes necessary to identify whom do you need in the process and who are not required at all.

5. **Communicating the Strategy:** Once the human resources are identified, the strategies must be communicated to them very clearly and precisely. They must understand why they are being involved and what role they have to play and also what is expected out of them. If these questions are answered positively, the performance management process can be effectively implemented in the organisation.

6. **Identifying Gaps and Monitoring the Progress:** When human resources are involved and their roles are clear to them, the strategic plan is put in front of them in

order to have holistic approach and generate as many views as possible. This helps to identify gaps, if any and monitor the progress of the performance management program.

3.3 Reasons for the Use of Advanced Performance Management Techniques

Performance management is the organisation's, department's and individual's important activity. This helps to manage and improve the performance of the individual and in a way of the organisation as a whole. This process is common across organisations and sectors, only depending upon the circumstance, external and internal factors, the nature of implementation of performance management process changes. Give below are the reasons for advancement of using performance management techniques in the organisation:

1. **Advancement in Management:** The role of management has changed over a period of time. It is not just managing the men but also developing resources for the betterment of organisations and individuals.
2. **Technology:** With technological upgradations, it has become very important that the organisations have competent human resources for using the latest technology. Hence the need for performance management has evolved.
3. **Market Forces:** Every organisation, these days has become performance oriented and all try to create high performance work systems for themselves. In order to remain in competition and to beat competition, the performance of the employees must be managed in such a way that they help organisations to create and maintain competitive advantage for themselves.
4. **Industrial Relations:** In order to maintain better human relations at work and eliminate conflicts and disagreements, the employees need to be performance oriented. When employees concentrate on improving their performance, they tend to forget the issues related to disagreements and conflicts.

3.4 Top Management Agreement, Commitment and Leadership

It is very important to know that however critical the process is, if it is not approved by the management, it could not be implemented in the organisation. Hence, in order to start any initiative in the organisation, it must be supported by the top management.

Managers play a key role in the entire performance management activity. They are responsible for overall development of the employee. Activities like scheduling training and development initiatives, conducting performance appraisal, having evaluation criteria set etc. are some of the important roles plays by

The success or failure of the performance management system in the organisation depends upon the support provided by top management. If top management is committed to the performance development of the employees, then only this initiative can fetch favourable results for the organisation as well as individual.

3.4.1 Role of Top Managers in Performance Management

In modern times, corporate leadership provides assistance on a number of issues, from strategic objectives to short-term goals. Top management must set achievable standards for work performance in the short and long terms. Top managers remind employees that they should not rest in peace until and unless the organisation has achieved competitive advantage in the market.

1. **Operating Responsibilities:** Top managers in the organisation have operating responsibilities to execute. They must provide the operating framework to the organisation that includes the goals for the time and the way in which they need to be achieved. These must be done with utmost tact and the top management must see to it that everyone in the organisation is comfortable with the framework provided by the top management. In short, top managers in this context must provide good leadership to the entire organisation.

2. **Strategy Formulation and Implementation:** Top management is involved in strategy formulation, and implementation, activities to inspire in employees for the attitude necessary to beat the heavy competition. This can be achieved through top leadership's strategic initiatives containing detailed training on of how to produce top-quality products, have utmost customer satisfaction, increase the current market share, and secure long-term profitability.

3. **Involve in Competency Work:** It is necessary for the top managers to be involved in competency based work. As implementation of performance management is the top down approach and they are the source of leadership for the employees working under them. Hence improving the competencies of the other top managers and thereby enhancing the competencies of the employees working under them must be the main task of top management. This enables the measurement and improvement of the performance effective.

4. **Provide Employees with SMART Goals:** In order to reach the strategic goals, and achieve the vision and mission of the organisation, the employees must be provided

with certain short term and long term goals. This will enable the employees to understand the bigger picture slowly and they will not get confused regarding the level of output expected out of them. At the same time, the top management must see to it that the goals set by them must be SMART that means, Specific, Measurable, Achievable, Realistic and Time bound.

5. **Other Responsibilities**

   (a) Top management must communicate the vision and mission statements to the employees and also explain them how to translate the statements in to the short term and long term goals.

   (b) They must also state the work expectations to the employees and clearly communicate what management is expecting out of them. This clarity makes the employees accountable for their work and their performance can be managed effectively.

   (c) The top management must inform the employees about their progress towards the goal accomplishment. As the employees do not always get to see the larger picture, they can see a small size of the goal that is set for them or for the department as a whole. Management must keep the employees informed whether their performance is as per the standards or it needs further improvements.

   (d) Top management must inculcate the feeling of shared beliefs among the employees. This helps the top management to have continuous performance evaluation and continuous performance management in the organisation.

3.4.2 Role of Line Managers in Performance Management

The line managers or the front line management play a very central role in implementing performance management policies. Thus, it becomes very important for the top management to understand whether line managers have the clarity about the process of performance management and also they have desired level of competencies to execute the performance management process. Some line managers might not understand the seriousness of the process and be very casual towards the execution of the activity. Listed below are the roles that they are supposed to do, in order to avoid confusion if any.

- Line managers must provide supportive leadership to the employees and seek guidance from top management about the same. They must act as a connecting link between the top management and the employees.

- They must communicate with other line managers and understand their issues or progress about the performance management process and together decide further plan of action and goals for the team.
- Their main focus must be on simplifying the process of performance management so that employees and other managers are able to understand their role in it.
- The line managers must ensure that the process is continuous and there are no breakages in the system to avoid future pending work. Continuous process includes regular performance reviews and regular feedback.

3.5 Building Performance Oriented Work Culture

Organisations today are constantly struggling to be in the competition to create and maintain the competitive advantage for them. As of today, access to latest technology and research and development facilities are not deciding factors as to who would stay in the competition and who could not. There is something more to it. And the answer for this is having strong high performance work culture that enables the employees to constantly improve their performance and make the organisation a learning organisation. Quality of employees working in the organisation and their efforts in the overall achievement of strategic objectives make the organisation to stay in the competition for a longer period of time.

Sustainability of the performance associated organisation culture is reliant on the capability of an organisation to cultivate talent for significant contribution in large roles in future. In order to ensure that the people are extremely capable of handling the toughest tasks that are allotted to them and the leadership in pipeline is equally strong and competent; organisations must take the performance review process very seriously and on continuous basis. Taking performance review always provides a timely feedback and early detection of competency gaps is possible. Early detection of gaps facilitates early cure and the performance management can happen fast and growth happens at an early stage.

Corporate culture represents accepted rules that they seem so natural and routine to the employees to the extent that they consider it as a part of their daily life and finds it extremely difficult to describe. It is nothing but the heart and soul of the organisation; including knowledge, beliefs, values and attitudes. It constantly guides the employees' thoughts on the issues like quality, customers, teamwork, innovation and decision making. These all have an impact on company's performance in some or the other way. This directly has an impact on productivity and the revenue of the organisation.

The corporate culture very well deserves the attention of all the employees in order to bring remarkable changes in the performance of the organisation as a whole. Let us now look at the various steps followed by companies these days to build performance oriented work culture.

1. **Define the Behaviour:** The culture must clearly define what it expects from the employees. As it is mentioned in the earlier paragraph, that the employees consider the organisation culture very natural and routine in the similar way, corporate culture must be designed in such a way that it states the expected level of behavior of the employees. That is how the employees must behave in the organisation in order to improve the performance level.

2. **Establish Best Practices:** Organizational culture must always try to establish quality practices and processes in the organisation. When the culture lays down best practices, the employees automatically become performance oriented and very little is left to the top management for review and monitor. The organisational culture must be OCTAPACE in nature which simply means: There must be Openness, Confrontation, Trust, Authenticity, Proactiveness, Autonomy, Collaboration and Experimentation as elements of organisation culture. This ultimately leads to higher level of performance.

3. **Communicate, Train and Coach Employees:** The organisational culture must provide for transparent and open communication channels. The more communication happens, the more chances are of performance development. Employees can seek the help of their managers and receive true and constructive response for further development. Whenever necessary the organisation must be open to mentor and coach the employees for achievement of their personal goals and achieve the ladders in the career path. This increases the commitment and belongingness of the employees towards the organisation.

4. **Align Organisational Rewards and Recognition:** Employees need something in return to the amount of performance that they have shown towards the goal achievement of the organisation. If they are not adequately rewarded, monetarily or non-monetarily, they might feel less motivated and that has a direct impact on their productivity and consequently on the performance levels. To avoid this, the corporate culture must align organisational rewards and recognition policies to the performance management activity.

3.6 Factors Affecting the Effective Use of Performance Management

Performance management system is the most critical part in the organisation and hence it must be implemented with utmost care and knowledge. But at the same time, this process involves the entire organisation involving human and non-human resources and hence there is a possibility that they might have an impact on the use and implementation of performance management in the organisation. The factors affecting the effective use of performance management are listed below:

3.6.1 Design

The performance management system must be designed in such a way that it is in sync with the organisational structure. It is actually advisable to have existing employees of the organisation to be a part of designing performance management system for the organisation. If employees are made part of the designing section, they will better understand the process followed in the organisation, at the same time the managers will not have to spend extra time in explaining them the process of performance management. But if this system is not designed properly i.e. the goals established for this process are not related to the organisation's strategic goals, then this system might not work well for the organisation in the long run. While designing the performance management system, the existing structure of the organisation, reporting relationships, processes and policies etc. must be given more importance in order to have desired level of results.

3.6.2 Training

Training is another critical factor that affects the effectiveness of performance management system. A study has shown that if managers are using a particular tool for appraising the performance of the employee, they must receive complete training as to how the tool needs to be used and how the results could be generated. If the rater himself is not aware of the rating scale and their implications, the purpose of performance management will not be served. The training in this regards involves explaining the use of performance appraisal methods, documenting the records of employees for further appropriate use, communicating the feedback to the employees in a constructive manner and helping them further to manage their performance in order to meet career goals and strategic goals of the organisation and of self. Hence, if training is not provided to the managers, it can affect the effectiveness of the performance management system.

3.6.3 Employee Development

The main objective of the performance management system must be to develop the performance of the employees rather than focusing on the administrative goals like pay raises and incentives etc. When the development of the employees is made the focus point, it automatically results into salary hike and other related benefits. But when the employee is told that he is going to receive benefits, then it might happen that he/she always expects something in return and focus only on getting rewards instead of focusing on the performance management. If the goals are not made clear to the employees as to why performance management is important for them, the employee development might prove to be the most important factor affecting the effective use of performance management.

3.6.4 Corporate Culture

Corporate culture basically defines the way employees complete their tasks and their relationships with others in the organisation. The corporate culture comprises of values, beliefs, trusts, rituals that are followed by the people working in a particular organisation. Culture always brings everything together. Organizational culture has a changeable impact on the employee's performance levels and motivational levels. Employees work really harder if they consider themselves a part of the corporate culture and vice-versa. The corporate culture, thus must be adopted by everyone in a similar manner in order to get the desired results. Otherwise the performance levels of all the employees working in the same environment would be different and may not contribute to the final output in an expected way.

3.6.5 Review and Update

This is the last but the most powerful factor affecting the effective use of performance management system. If employees do not receive satisfactory review of their performance and subsequent update or feedback on the way they are performing, it is very likely that they lose their interest in the system and might no co-operate with full heart. Losing employee support in the process of performance management is not a good sign for the organisation as for growth, development and expansion, help of competent personnel is very much needed. If this review and update process is not followed religiously, employees might not be committed to the process.

Points to Remember

- Process of Implementing Performance Management
    1. Clarify Objectives
    2. Secure Senior Manager Buy-in
    3. Prepare System and Supporting Materials and Documentation
    4. Ensure Managers are Trained
    5. Ensure all Participant Employees are Trained
    6. Launch with Champion
    7. Monitor and Review Success
- Keys to a Successful Performance Management System
    1. Communicate Expectations
    2. Involve Employees in the Process
    3. Use a Systematic Approach
    4. Be Willing to Work Hard
    5. Make a Commitment to Success
- Challenges in Implementing Performance Management
    1. Lack of Alignment
    2. Lack of Measurements
    3. Leadership and Management Commitment
    4. Managing of the Performance System
    5. Managing Poor Performances
- Strategies for Effective Implementation of Performance Management
    1. Define the Need
    2. Determining Strategy
    3. Aligning Business Strategy with Performance Management Strategy
    4. Selection of Resources
    5. Communicating the Strategy
    6. Identifying Gaps and Monitoring the Progress
- Factors Affecting the Effective Use of Performance Management
    1. Training
    2. Employee Development
    3. Corporate Culture
    4. Review and Update

Questions for Discussion

1. Explain the process and guidelines for implementation of Performance Management System.
2. Discuss the strategies involved in effective implementation of performance management system.
3. Discuss the role of Top management agreement, commitment and leadership in Performance Management System.
4. What are the factors in building performance oriented work culture?
5. Explain the factors affecting of performance management.

Project Questions

1. How would you describe your organisation's culture? How supportive do you think the culture is for implementing a performance management system? What can you do to take advantage of a supportive culture?
2. What factor a manager should keep in mind while implementing new performance management system within the organisation?

Chapter 4...

Reward for Performance

Contents ...

4.1 Introduction
4.2 Reward System
    4.2.1 Objectives of Reward System
    4.2.2 Components of Reward System
    4.2.3 Elements of Employee Reward
    4.2.4 Linkage of Performance Management to Reward and Compensation System
4.3 Pitfalls of Performance Management
4.4 Remedies for Pitfalls of Performance Management
4.5 Concept of Performance Appraisal
    4.5.1 Definitions of Performance Appraisal
    4.5.2 Objectives of Performance Appraisal
    4.5.3 Features of Performance Appraisal
    4.5.4 Process of Performance Appraisal
    4.5.5 Performance Appraisal Methods
    4.5.6 Factors Necessary for a Performance Appraisal Policy
    4.5.7 Efficiencies of Performance Appraisal
    4.5.8 Limitations or Shortcomings of Performance Appraisal
    4.5.9 Guidelines for Performance Appraisal and Good Practices
    4.5.10 Good Practices of Performance Management in the Organisation
- Points to Remember
- Questions for Discussion
- Project Questions

Learning Objectives ...
- To understand the meaning, components and objectives of reward system
- To be able to explain the linkage between performance to reward and compensation system
- To learn the performance management pitfalls and remedies for the pitfalls
- To be able to understand the efficiencies and limitations of performance appraisal system
- To learn the guidelines for performance appraisal

4.1 Introduction

In the modern era of globalisation and techno-organisations, the concept of pay performance has started getting new dimensions. The basic idea behind having a reward system included in the performance management system is improving the efficiency of the employees. When employees come to know that their performance is going to be rewarded either monetarily or non-monetarily, the level of performance displayed by them changes and each one of them tries to earn more and more rewards by enhancing his/her performance. Efficiency level of the employees is determined by comparing actual performance with standard performance. And by measuring the performance level, the criteria of rewards are decided.

Rewards system in the organisation basically deals with the policies, processes, strategies and functions in the organisation which guarantee that the contributions made by employees towards the goal achievement of the organisation are recognised by all means and there is no confusion regarding the rewards to be given. The chief goal of a reward system is to increase people's willingness to work in the organisation, increase their level of commitment or belongingness towards the organisation by enhancing the overall productivity of the employees. Research on motivation shows that extrinsic rewards, such as pay, can be effective motivators when clearly and strongly related to performance management.

4.2 Reward System

Performance Management system performs the most important function in the organisation i.e. of measuring and managing the performance of the employees; which in turn contributes towards the organisation's growth strategy. A reward system is a system that is designed to determine the amount of pay to be given to the employees as against their qualification, experience and performance (past / current). The main objective of the reward system must be to motivate the employees in the organisation.

Rewards System is the programme initiated and implemented by the organisations to reward performance and motivate employees on individual and/or group levels. They are normally apart from salaries, but may be monetary in nature. Motivated and efficient employees are the backbone of any organisation's success. A motivated and efficient employee enables the organisation to maintain competitive advantage in the market. An effective reward system must be linked with performance management which focuses on improving the performance of the employees, performance based pay and offer a lot of opportunities for the organisation as well as the employees to learn and better the performance from the last quarter.

A well-organised and well planned reward system may have a favourable impact on the performance of the employees in many ways for example, imbibing the sense of ownership in the minds of the employees. This will facilitate long term focus with continuous improvement; it will also reduce service costs, encourages team work, and lowers employee frustration in the overall performance of the company.

Rewards can be the most important source of motivation and encouragement for the employees. The only thing to be kept in the mind is the strategies behind implementing a particular reward system and it must be managed under true conditions.

4.2.1 Objectives of Reward System

Due to the intense competition outside, companies now-a-days are trying really hard to retain employees in their organisation. It is the employees who can take the organisation to the next level and help achieve the objectives of profit maximisation. In this case, rewards play a vital role in improving the morale and motivation of the employees. Given below are the few more objectives of a reward system.

1. **Improving Organisational Culture:** It is always said that culture of the organisation and rewards go hand in hand. Organizational culture talks mainly about the way people behave in organisations, their working relationships, who and by whom the decisions are to be made etc. On the other hand, rewards decide the financial returns an individual gets for the amount of time, knowledge, skills he/she invests for the growth and development of the company. So we can say that the culture of the organisation and the rewards system have direct relation. And changing just one of them is going to affect the other very hard. Hence, in order to bring a win-win situation and get favourable results, it is strongly recommended that there should be a concrete reward system in the organisation so that employees are relaxed on the financial terms and then create a complimentary organisational culture so that employees are motivated and happy on the career development front also.

2. **Increasing Customer Focus:** This is the most important objective behind having a reward system in the organisation. Customers are regarded as king. This is simply because increasing customer base is going to create a lot of goodwill for the organisation and at the same time increase the revenue for it. Like it is mentioned in the above point, if you want your employees to be at peace and feel committed to the organisation, they must get something in return for the skills and time they invest in your organisation. Thus, if you want your employees to bring more and more customers for you, the presence of a favourable reward system plays a vital role in this. When an employee feels that he/she is getting enough as per the amount of work he/she has done, they concentrate more on their work and try and get more rewards. This increases their relationship with the organisation and they feel more loved and cared.

3. **Attraction and Retention:** It is always noticed that who is attracted towards your organisation and who would work for your organisation depends largely upon the kind of reward system you have. It is also observed that a high reward leads to high satisfaction and as a result low turnover. This is simply because those who are happy with their current rewards may not want to leave the organisation and can be retained successfully. The objective here is to design the reward system in such a way that it aims at retaining the most valuable employees in the organisation. The emphasis here is to focus on the external competition. The rewards offered in one organisation must be competitive with an other organisation. This practice helps to attract and retain talent in the organisation through effective use of a reward system.
4. **Motivation of Performance:** Employees always perform as per the expectations of the organisation when they know that their performance is being valued and will be rewarded appropriately. This feeling motivates them and makes them sincere at work. This tool is used to generate that behaviour from the employees that leads to desired outcomes. For instance, employees have expectancy that if they produce 10 units of a product, they will receive normal amount of pay. But if they produce 15 units of product, they will receive their normal pay plus some bonus. And this thinking itself makes them work beyond their limits and motivates them to the core.

4.2.2 Components of Reward System

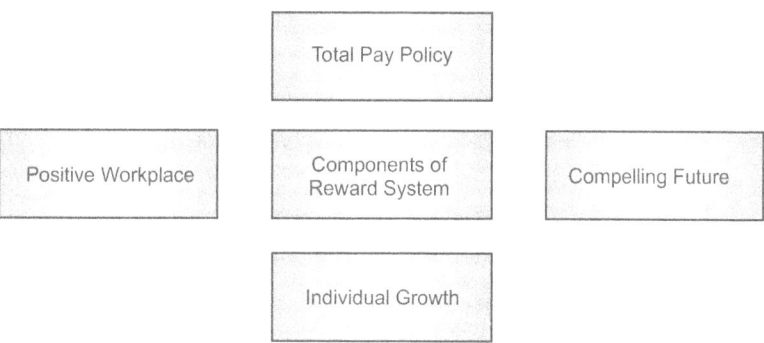

Fig. 4.1: Component of Reward System

1. **Individual Growth:** In order to make the reward system work as per the expectations of the management, it is very important to take into consideration the individual growth of the employees. And hence, investing in people becomes the fundamental

aspect of any reward system. Investment in people makes them knowledge wise and skill wise independent. Also there are less chances of committing a mistake which saves on wastages. Individual growth can be achieved by imparting training and development activities to the employees. When any individual is given training, it is the responsibility of the organisation to keep a track whether he is benefited out of it or not. This helps the organisation in turn to manage the performance of the employees and provide them with appropriate rewards.

2. **Compelling Future:** The future of the organisation depends on the employees. By keeping this in mind the organisation or the management, must be transparent enough to set SMART standards for the employees. By SMART we mean, Specific, Measureable, Achievable, Reasonable and Time bound. For this, it is very important that the vision and mission of the organisation are communicated to the employees. When the standards are clear, the employees can better perform what is expected out of them and appropriate reward can be given to them.

3. **Positive Workplace:** This is one of the important aspects of a reward system. To have a fair and transparent reward system, the organisation's climate and culture must be suitable and positive. The focus and the only aim of the organisation must be development of its people. In short, it must be people centric rather than money or process centric. And hence all the efforts relating to them must be adopted. The first thing is providing transformational leadership to them. This not only achieves their commitment at workplace but also passes on the legacy of a leader follower in the organisation.

4. **Total Pay:** This is a concept that includes fixed pay, basic pay and variable pay. The very concept of variable pay suggests that, when an employee performs better, he is eligible for extra rewards. This boosts the morale of the employees to perform beyond their limits. This activity does not only improve the performance of the individual but also of the organisation as a whole.

4.2.3 Elements of Employee Reward

1. **Base Pay**

Base (or basic) pay is the level of pay (the fixed salary or wage) that constitutes the rate for the job. It may provide the platform for determining additional payments related to performance, competence or skill. It may also govern pension entitlement and life insurance. The basic levels of pay for jobs reflect both internal and external relativities.

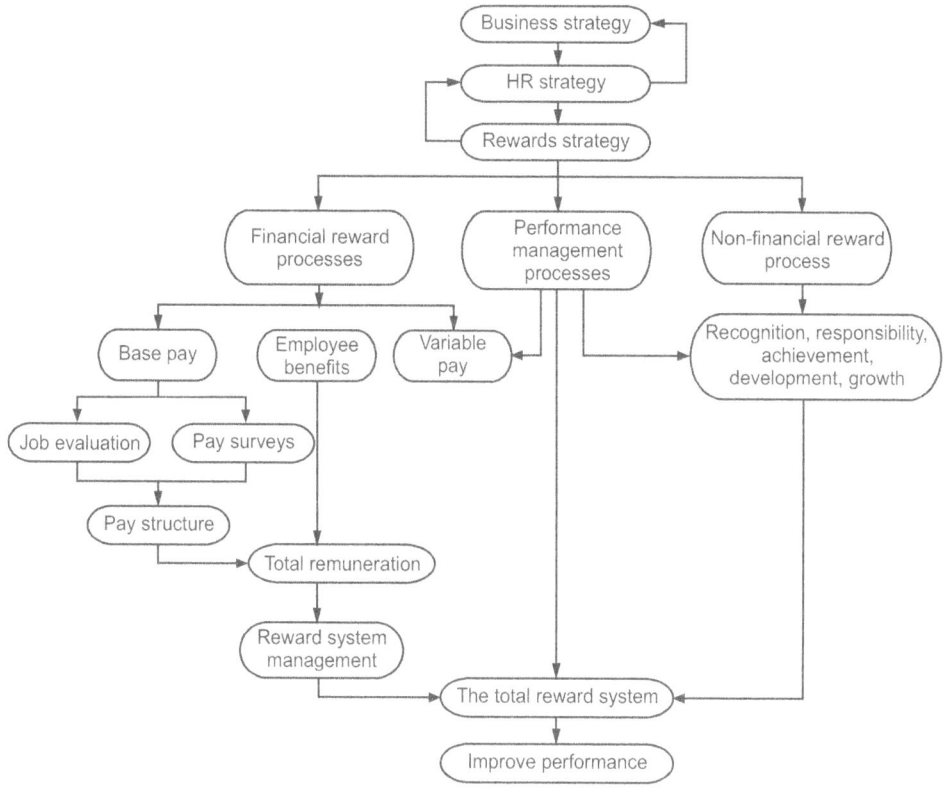

Fig. 4.2

The internal relativities may be measured by some form of job evaluation which places jobs in a hierarchy (although the trend now is to play down the notion of hierarchy in the new process-based organisations).

External relativities are assessed by tracking market rates.

Alternatively, levels of pay may be agreed through negotiation: by collective bargaining with trade unions or by reaching individual agreements. The base rate for a job is sometimes regarded as the rate for a competent or skilled person in that job. Such a rate may be varied in a skill-based or competence-based system according to the individual's skill or competence.

Levels of pay may be based on long-standing structures the origins of which are shrouded in the mists of time and which have been updated in response to movements in market rates and inflation, and through negotiations. In many organisations pay levels evolve – they are not planned or maintained systematically. Rates are fixed by managerial judgement of what is required to recruit and retain people. They may be adjusted in response to individual or collective pressure for increases or upgradings. This evolutionary and ad hoc process can result in a chaotic and illogical pay structure which is inequitable, leads to inconsistent and unfair decisions and is difficult to understand, expensive to maintain and the cause of dissatisfaction and demotivation.

Base pay may be expressed as an annual, weekly or hourly rate. This can be termed a time-rate or time-based payment system. Such systems are simple but they can be made more complex by the addition of various kinds of allowances such as overtime or shift payments. Time rates may be 'spot rates' – i.e. comprising one rate for the job – or there may be a range of pay for each job grade in which progression takes place according to time in the job, performance, competence and/or skill. The rate may be adjusted to reflect increases in the cost of living or market rates by the organisation unilaterally or by agreement with a trade union. Service-related, performance, skill-based or competence-related pay increases may be added to, or 'consolidated' into, the basic rate, and these form the basis for pension contributions, sick pay, payment for overtime, and bonuses or profit shares when these are awarded as a percentage of base pay.

2. Contingent Pay

Additional financial rewards may be provided that are related to performance, competence, contribution, skill and/or experience. These are referred to as 'contingent pay'. If such payments are not consolidated into base pay, they can be described as 'variable pay'. Variable pay is sometimes defined as 'pay at risk'. For example, the pay of sales representatives on a 'commission-only' basis is entirely at risk. The main types of contingent pay are:

(a) **Individual performance-related pay** – in which increases in base pay or cash bonuses are determined by performance assessment and ratings (also known as merit pay).

(b) **Bonuses** – rewards for successful performance which are paid as cash (lump) sums related to the results obtained by individuals, teams or the organisation.

(c) **Incentives** – payments linked with the achievement of previously set targets which are designed to motivate people to achieve higher levels of performance; the targets are usually quantified in such terms as output or sales.

(d) **Commission** – a special form of incentive in which sales representatives are paid on the basis of a percentage of the sales value they generate.

(e) **Service-related pay** – which increases by fixed increments on a scale or pay spine depending on service in the job; there may sometimes be scope for varying the rate of progress up the scale according to performance.

(f) **Competence-related pay** – which varies according to the level of competence achieved by the individual.

(g) **Contribution-related pay** – which relates pay to both outputs (performance) and inputs (competence).

(h) **Skill-based pay (sometimes called knowledge-based pay)** – which varies according to the level of skill the individual achieves.

(i) **Career development pay** – which rewards people for taking on additional responsibilities as their career develops laterally within a broad grade (a broad banded pay structure).

3. **Allowances**

Allowances are elements of pay in the form of a separate sum of money for such aspects of employment as overtime, shift working, call-outs and living in Mumbai or other large cities. Large-city allowances are sometimes consolidated: organisations which are simplifying their pay structure may 'buy out' the allowance and increase base pay accordingly.

4. **Total Earnings**

Total earnings are usually calculated as the sum of base pay and any additional payments.

5. **Employee Benefits**

Employee benefits, also known as indirect pay, include pensions, sick pay, insurance cover and company cars. They comprise elements of remuneration additional to the various forms of cash pay and also include provisions for employees that are not strictly remuneration, such as annual holidays.

6. **Total Remuneration**

Total remuneration is the value of all cash payments (total earnings) and benefits received by employees.

7. **Non-Financial Rewards**

Non-financial rewards include any rewards which focus on the need people perceive to varying degrees for achievement, recognition, responsibility, influence and personal growth.

The elements of a reward system and their interrelationships are illustrated in Fig. 4.1. But they can be combined in many different ways. There is no ideal pattern for a reward system.

4.2.4 Linkage of Performance Management to Reward and Compensation System

The word performance has a lot of weightage in the organisation setup. Organisations are expected to perform up to the mark in order to survive against competition and beat the competition. And for the organisation to perform well, it is very important that the people working in the organisation are performing beyond their limits.

Performance management can be defined as a continuous process of assessing and measuring the performance of an individual and aligning it with organisational goals. And it is the most important job of the HR department. Performance management is widely used in all organisations across various sectors only for a simple reason that if performance is not measured, there would be no feedback on the progress, if there is no feedback, employees will not understand where they stand in the organisation and what is expected out of them and hence the objective of the organisation of growth and development will become difficult to achieve. In a marketing firm, for example, the number of sales in a day is the deciding factor or a standard set for sales professionals, wherein their performance is assessed by the number of sales they are able to make. Hence if they are unable to meet standards, the feedback must be shared with them, they must know how to improve their performance etc. due to this, it is very important to have a performance management system in the picture.

Similarly as performance management is important, rewarding performance is also equally important. And a reward system is an integral part of the performance management system. There are two main branches of performance management: feedback system and reward system. Feedback system mainly focuses on aligning performance with organisational goals whereas reward system deals with motivation and continuous improvement of employees. The reward system basically deals with giving something in return to the employees, in monetary or non-monetary form. The traditional approach of reward system was very different than it is today. Previously the rewards were based on the job description i.e., the position which the person is holding, he/ she used to receive the rewards in comparison to that. There was no role of performance. Even if the employee performs exceptionally well, he would receive the reward in capacity of the position he holds. But this approach doesn't exist now-a-days and employees have started receiving rewards purely on the basis of their performance.

Why link reward system to performance management system?

To make the system work in the long run it is very necessary that it is linked with other functions and processes in the organisation. When the two systems are run together and simultaneously, it becomes easier for the organisation to decide the objectives and sustain in the market for a longer period of time. The bond or connection between rewards and performance helps the organisation to retain the employee in the organisation as well as ensure his/her commitment at the workplace. This automatically improves the contribution capacity of the employee. Employees must perform well in order to be rewarded is the most widely used approach and commonly it is called as "pay for performance". Apart from the normal pay which is called as base pay, that a person gets by default, there is another pay that is introduced in the reward system and that is variable pay which solely depends upon the performance level displayed by the employee.

At the same time, we should not forget the motivation theory shared by F. Herzberg. According to him both, hygiene and motivational factors are responsible for the mental well-being of an employee. And hence, a good reward-performance linked system should look at the motivational factors also along with the hygiene factors. In simple words, the employee will not be motivated by mere money; he/she seeks recognition, appreciation by seniors etc. which should be provided to him/her from time to time to improve the morale. Both these types of reward systems ensure higher motivation, retention, employee engagement and job satisfaction.

Benefits of Performance Based Reward System

An effective performance based reward system generates a lot of positive outcomes for the organisation. The same are mentioned below:

1. Decreased attrition rate
2. Motivates employees to perform better
3. Increased employee involvement
4. Existence of healthy competition
5. Enhancement of knowledge, skills and attitude

4.3 Pitfalls of Performance Management

Performance management is the most talked about process of the human resource department, as it is believed that the success and failure of the organisation largely depends on the way people behave and perform against the standards set. However in spite of the highest degree of care the taken during the performance management process, there are certain limitations that are faced. Below are the reasons why performance management fails in the organisation:

1. **Achievement of Targets:** This is mainly related with the lenient and casual attitude that the employees have towards the target set for them. This in turn affects the overall performance management activity of the organisation. This failure occurs mainly because the standards that are set for the employees are ambiguous and employees don't clearly understand what exactly is expected out of them. And when the assessment of the performance is going on there is a possibility that the situation becomes full of debate, disagreements and chaos. To avoid this, every organisation must set SMART goals for its employees and by SMART we mean, Specific, Measurable, Achievable, Realistic and Time bound. This makes the before and after stage of performance management simpler.

2. **Lack of Integration:** Performance management is an integrated approach and it must be implemented in the same way in the organisation. There must be a synergy between performance management strategy and other strategic aspects of the organisation. Performance management system cannot succeed on its own, strategic objectives, strategic planning must be harmonised to have a collective effort and the performance management system can be effectively used.

3. **Lack of Leadership Support:** The implementation of the performance management system needs the support of the top management. And it must be driven by leadership and management. The leadership must be implemented with the commitment of implementing the performance management system in the organisation. If this support is not there, the system cannot be implemented effectively. Organizations having a strong performance oriented culture have strong values that results in better and enhanced productivity.
4. **Lack of Rewards:** A reward system that encourages high performance and discourages low and mediocre performance must be put in place. This encourages all the employees to follow the system religiously and be eligible for the rewards. However absence of such a reward system will definitely lead to failure of the performance management system. There would not be any motivation to the employees for following the system. Much emphasis of the rewards must be on the non-monetary rewards as it increases the motivational level. And consequently results into higher output.
5. **Lack of Monitoring:** Performance management system needs regular monitoring and check-up. Problems and grey areas in the system must be identified at an early stage in order to strengthen the performance process. Monitoring and check-up helps the organisation to collect the information, analyse and interpret it. This information can be further used for appropriate purposes.
6. **Lack of Evaluation:** This is the most crucial factor responsible for failure of the performance management system. This helps to detect the problem at a very early stage and ensures quick action to the problem identified. The performance management system must be regularly monitored and evaluated. The success or failure of the entire performance management system depends upon this factor.
7. **Design Challenges:** The performance management system must be designed in such a way that it addresses particular problems or needs of the organisation. The people who are involved in designing the performance management system must possess a high level of competence and must have a thorough knowledge of the organisation for which the system is being designed. Having an incomplete and incompetent system leads to loss of credibility, time, resources, costs, and it also adds to increased resistance of people towards change.
8. **Implementation Failure:** Even if the system is designed perfectly, the main challenge lies with the implementation part. Leaders in the organisation need to manage couple of run time issues while implementing the performance management system in the organisation. This should be a continuous activity and must be remembered to not to conduct it just once or twice a year. Also the performance feedback must be timely and true.

4.4 Remedies for Pitfalls of Performance Management

1. Design
- Consultation
- Testing/ piloting
- Design expertise

2. Integration
- Strategic plan
- HR, culture, structure
- Intradepartmental, interdepartmental and intersectoral

3. Leadership
- Commitment
- Competence
- Vision
- Inspiration

10. Evaluation
- Regular periods
- Continuous development

Integrated Performance Management System

4. Competence
- Knowledge, attitude and skills
- Development of indicators
- Communication

9. Monitoring
- Continuous process
- Early warning
- Corrective action

5. Implementation
- Change management
- Professionalism
- Time management
- Documentation

8. Communication
- Continuous
- Proactive
- Developmental feedback

7. Reward System
- Reward high performers
- Discourage mediocrity
- Promote non-monetary rewards

6. Motivation
- Organisational development
- Continuous process
- Sustainable

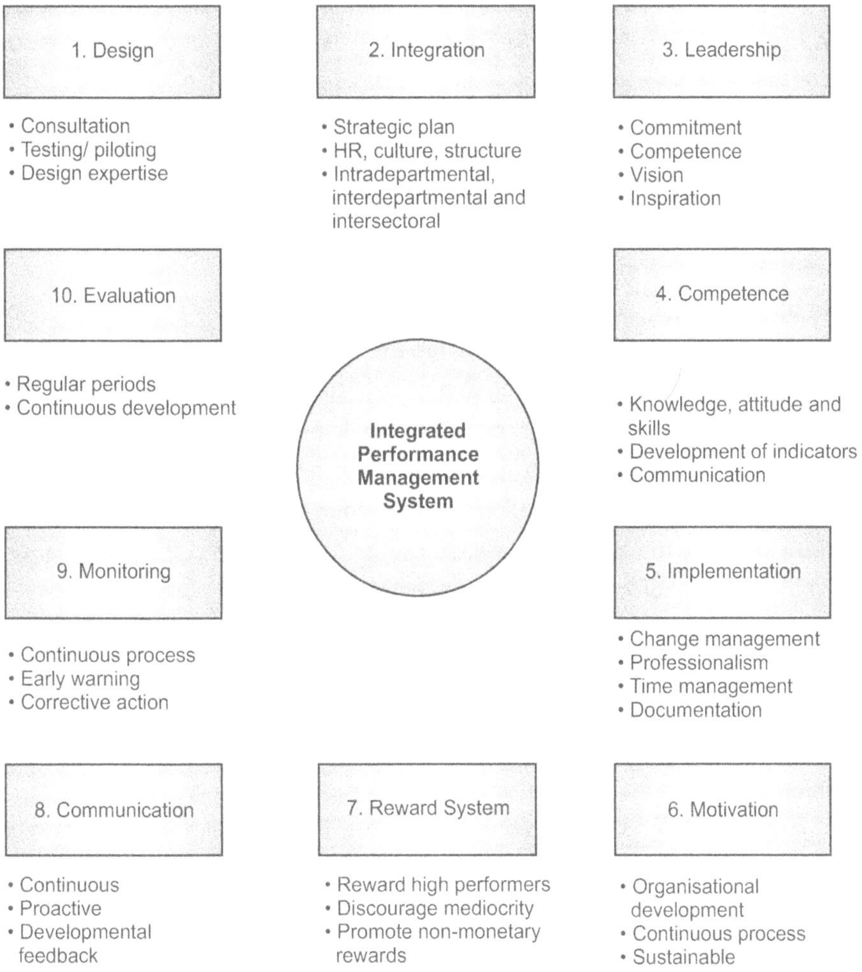

Fig. 4.3

1. **Design:** The reward system must be designed or re-designed in such a way that all the standards are very clear and transparent to all the employees. This will help them to improve their performance and eliminate deficiencies if any.

2. **Integration:** The rewards system must be integrated with the strategic, departmental, and organisational objectives. If it is not integrated, the employees would be confused to understand the objectives set and as a result expected level of performance would not be achieved and hence the reward system may fail as a whole.

3. **Leadership:** In order to successfully achieve individual and organisational goals and be eligible for additional rewards, better mentoring or leadership must be provided. A leader helps his followers in achieving the desired level of performance through constant feedback and goal sharing. This helps to strengthen the reward system of the organisation.
4. **Competence:** Competence basically talks about the KSAs (Knowledge, Skills and Attitudes) of the employees. The rewards system must be designed in such a way that it helps the individual increase his knowledge base, develop the right kind of attitude and enhance the skills level.
5. **Implementation:** Just the way, the designing of the reward system is important, similarly the implementation of the reward system has a major role to play. If the reward system is not implemented in an expected way, the performance evaluation and performance management cannot be regulated properly in the organisation.
6. **Motivation:** It must be remembered that the reward system of the organisation should be a source of motivation for the employees, because when the employees are motivated, the entire organisation can be developed and the performance level of the organisation can be taken to the next level.
7. **Reward System:** The reward system of the organisation should be encouraging enough so that all the employees would be interested in performing beyond their limits just to get additional rewards. The rewards should be monetary as well as non-monetary and the targets set for the rewards should not be too complicated or impractical.
8. **Communication:** Communication is the most important part in any activity in the organisation. Without communication almost all the processes will fail. Right from designing the reward system till the implementation, every little aspect must be communicated to the employees across the organisation. Transparency in communication improves the chances of better performance and commitment towards the organisation.
9. **Monitoring:** Supervision or monitoring is also an important aspect of reward system. Supervision helps employees understand their mistakes in run time, also it is kind of an on-the-job training provided by the supervisor to the employees. Hence this is a must.
10. **Evaluation:** The performance evaluation measures must be open and communicated to the employees. The openness in the system helps to improve the performance level and thereby achievement of targets.

4.5 Concept of Performance Appraisal

Performance appraisal is a method of evaluating the output of employees at the workplace, normally including both the qualitative and quantitative aspects of job performance. It is a systematic and objective way of evaluating work-related and behavioural aspects of employees. It is a process of establishing standards regarding employee performance at every level and matching individual performance to those standards.

Performance appraisal is the periodic and systematic assessment of the employees in terms of the performance, aptitude, capabilities and other qualities which are necessary for successfully carrying out their jobs. It is a systematic effort on the part of management and has a direct linkage with induction, selection, training etc. of the employees. It identifies areas where the employees need training and provides data to determine promotions, transfers, etc.

4.5.1. Definitions of Performance Appraisal

1. According to **Scott, Clothier and Spreigel:** *"A performance appraisal is the process of evaluation of an employee's performance of a job in terms of its requirements."*

2. According to **Alford and Beatty:** *"A performance appraisal is the evaluation or appraisal of the relative worth to the company of a man's service on his job."*

3. According to **Edwin B Flippo:** *"Performance appraisal is a systematic, periodic and so far as humanly possible, an impartial rating of an employee's excellence in matters pertaining to his present job and to his potentials for a better job."*

4. According to **Cummings:** *"The overall objective of performance appraisal is to improve the efficiency of an enterprise by attempting to mobilise the best possible efforts from individuals employed in it. Such appraisals achieve four objectives viz.:*
   - Salary reviews
   - Training and development of individuals
   - Planning job rotation
   - Assistance in promotions

5. **Wayne Cascio:** *"Performance appraisal is the systematic description of an employee's job relevant strengths and weaknesses".*

6. **Michael Crino:** *"Performance appraisal is the process of assessing quantitative and qualitative aspects of an employee's job performance".*

7. **Sexton Adams:** *"Performance appraisal is a method for management to make fair and impartial analysis of the value of employees to the organisation".*

8. **Prof. Dale Yoder:** *"Performance appraisal includes all formal procedures used to evaluate personalities and contributions and potentials of group members in a working organisation".*

   It is a continuous process to secure information necessary for making correct and objective decisions about employees".

9. **Prof. Mirza. S. Saiyadain:** According to *Prof. Mirza S. Saiyadain, "Performance appraisal could be seen as an objective method of judging the relative worth or ability of an individual employee in performing his tasks. If objectively done, the appraisal can help to identify a better worker from a poor one".*

   In this view of Prof. M. S. Saiyadain, the following are the two important aspects relating to performance appraisal.

   (a) It is an objective method of judging the relative worth or ability of an employee in performing his tasks.

   (b) A performance appraisal, as can make clear the relative strengths and weaknesses of an employee, if done objectively, helps to identify a better worker from poor one. This is important from the viewpoint of management to identify better workers/ employees for placing more responsibilities on the trusted workers/employees.

10. **Prof. Arun Monappa and Prof. Mirza Saiyadain:** Prof. Arun Monappa and Prof. Saiyadain have expressed their views on performance appraisal more comprehensively by giving suitable examples. Accordingly, appraisals and judgements regarding the characteristics, traits and performance of others are done. On the basis of these judgements, value of others can be assessed and what is good and what is bad also can be identified. In day-to-day life, a tailor, a doctor, an architect, a hair dresser, etc. is selected through the evaluation of his worth based on personal judgement.

    In the industrial field, according to them, performance appraisal is a systematic evaluation of employees/personnel by their superiors or supervisors of their performance. Such appraisals can be used for making various administrative decisions relating to selection, training, promotion, transfer, wage and salary administration, etc.

4.5.2 Objectives of Performance Appraisal

- **Maintaining an Inventory:** To enable an organisation to maintain inventory of the number and quality of all managers and to identify and meet their training needs and aspirations.

- **Initiating Personnel Development:** To initiate personnel development by having discussions with individual employees and line managers and identifying the reasons for faulty performance.
- **Improving the Employee Performance:** To suggest ways of improving the employee's performance when he is not found to be up to the mark.
- **Determine Rewards:** To determine increment rewards and provide a reliable index for promotions and transfers to positions of greater responsibility.
- **Suitable Training and Development:** To serve as a guide for formulating a suitable training and development programme. Performance appraisal can inform employees about their progress and tell them what skills they need to develop, to become eligible for pay raises or promotions or both.
- **Decision Making:** To help in taking decisions in respect of premature retirements or of giving extension in service to the employees.

Fig. 4.4: Objectives of Performance Appraisal

4.5.3 Features of Performance Appraisal

The important features of performance appraisal are as follows:
1. Performance appraisal is not only a technique or method but is also a systematic and continuous process.

2. In performance appraisal, periodic and systematic assessment of employees' performance is done. Appraisals are arranged periodically according to some definite plan.
3. This technique is used by the management to make fair and impartial analysis of the value of employees.
4. It is a systematic objective description of the employees' job relevant strengths and weaknesses.
5. In the process of performance appraisal, efforts are made to bring an uniformity while appraising the job performance of the employees working in an organisation.
6. Performance appraisal can be formal or informal. Informal performance appraisals are unplanned and are often just statements made in passing about an employee's performances. Most organisations use a formal appraisal system following a certain procedure to appraise the performances of their employees.
7. There are various objectives or purposes of doing appraisals of employees, but the important one is to find out how well the employees are performing their jobs and on that basis, to establish a plan of improvement.
8. Performance appraisal is different from job evaluation as well as merit rating.
9. There are different methods of appraising the performance of the employees. According to the objectives, suitable methods can be adopted.

4.5.4 Process of Performance Appraisal

Performance appraisal is planned, developed and implemented through a series of steps:

1. **Establish Performance Standards:** Appraisal systems require performance standards, which serve as benchmarks against which performance is to be measured. To be useful, standards should relate to the desired results of each job.
2. **Communicate the Standards:** Performance appraisal involves at least two parties, the appraiser who does the appraisal and the appraisee whose performance is to be evaluated, in order to make the appraisal process a success. The appraiser should prepare the job description clearly, help the appraisee set his goals and targets, analyse the results objectively, offer coaching and guidance to the appraisee whenever required and reward good results. The appraisee should be very clear about what he is doing and why he is doing it. Hence the performance standards must be communicated to the appraisees and their reactions should be noted down and if necessary the standards must be revised or modified.
3. **Measure Actual Performance:** After the performance standards are set and accepted, the next step is to measure the actual performance. This requires the use of dependable performance measures. Four measures commonly used by managers to measure actual performance are:
   - Personal observation
   - Statistical reports

- Oral reports
- Written reports

In order to be useful, the performance measures must be easy to use, reliable and able to report on critical behaviours that determine performance.

4. **Compare Actual Performance with the Standards:** Actual performance may be better than expected and sometimes it may go off the track. Whatever be the consequences, there should be a way to discuss and communicate the final outcome.
5. **Taking Corrective Action if Necessary:** Corrective action is of two types,
   - Immediate
   - Permanent

A combination of both the types of corrective actions may be initiated as the situation demands, to bring the individual's or group's or team's performance back on track. Corrective action may involve remedial training, counselling, mentoring, explanation of team goals, dispute and conflict resolution etc.

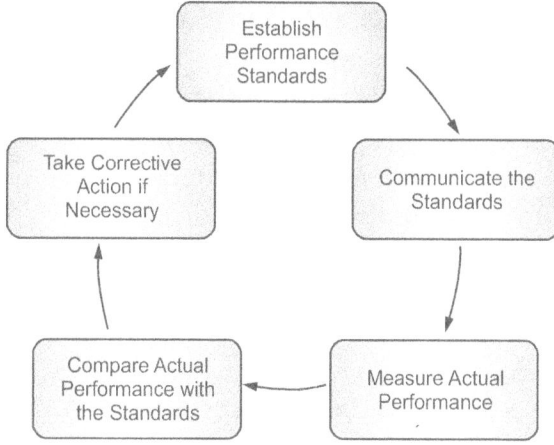

Fig. 4.5: Process of Performance Appraisal

4.5.5 Performance Appraisal Methods

Performance appraisal methods can be divided into two categories:
I. Past-oriented methods
II. Future-oriented methods

I. Past-oriented Methods

1. **Rating Scales:** The rating scale method is relatively easy to use, adjustable and cost effective. Employees' performance is rated on a rating scale based on performance criteria and almost all types of jobs can be evaluated with the rating scale. The

appraiser doesn't need any training to use the scale. Thus it helps to evaluate large number of employees within a short period of time. However appraisal may get affected adversely due to appraiser's biases which are particularly pronounced on subjective criteria such as cooperation, attitude and initiative. Also numerical scoring gives an illusion of precision which can't be proved in reality.

2. **Checklist:** Under this method a checklist of behavioural descriptions is prepared and each employee is evaluated against such a list. The appraiser just fills the checklist and a different staff member allocates weightages for each list and finally arrives at total points or marks obtained.

   Advantages:
   - The chances of bias are less as evaluation and recording is done by different persons. It makes comparison of two employees possible.

   Limitations:
   - This method is usually restricted only to staff of personnel department.
   - It is difficult to apply for all types of jobs.

3. **Forced Choice Method:** This also involves filling a checklist, however options are given to choose between two or more statements, all of which may be favourable or unfavourable. The appraiser is required to select the most appropriate statement that suits a particular employee. Here the appraiser does not know the desirable answer for a particular job. It is kept confidential in the 'key', stored in a computer. The answers of the rating are fed into the computer and marks are obtained with the help of keys.

   This method reduces subjectivity and establishes objective criteria of comparison between employees, but it does not involve the intervention of a third party.

   However it may lead to leniency i.e. clustering a large number of employees around a high point on a rating scale. This problem can be solved by compelling the appraiser to distribute the rates on all points on the rating scale.

4. **Critical Incidents Method:** This method is becoming very popular nowadays. It considers certain critical behaviours of an employee as evaluation criteria that make all the difference between effective and non-effective performance. The appraiser observes the employee's behaviour and records such critical incidents for evaluation in future.

5. **Behaviourally Anchored Rating Scales (BARS):** This method involves use of a rating scale whose scale points are determined by statements of effective and ineffective behaviours. It is also called as behavioural expectation scale. The scales

provide a series of descriptive statements of behaviour, ranging between the least to the most effective. The distinguishing features of BARS are listed below:

- Performance criteria are identified and defined by the people who are actually going to use the scales.
- The scales are based on actual and observable job behaviour that, represent specific levels of performance.
- BARS are specifically prepared for each job and are relevant to the job being evaluated.
- As the appraisers are actively involved in the research and development process, they are more likely to be committed to the final outcome.

6. **Field Review Method:** Under this method an appraisal is conducted by someone from other than the appraiser's department, typically by a person from the corporate office or the HR Department. The appraiser evaluates employee records and conducts appraisal discussion with his or her supervisor. The method is primarily used to decide whether to promote an employee at the managerial level. Field reviews are also useful when comparable information is needed from employees in different units or locations. A member of the HR Department or central administrative staff meets with a small group of appraisers from each supervisory unit and goes over each employee's rating with them to:

- Identify areas of inter-appraiser disagreement
- Help the group arrive at a consensus and
- Determine that each appraiser interprets the standards similarly

7. **Performance Tests and Observations:** This method can be followed where there are a limited number of jobs. Appraisal is done by conducting a test of employee's knowledge or skills. The test may be in the form of a written or an actual demonstration of skills. However due to the nature of this method, it measures employee's potential performance rather than the actual performance. The test needs to be reliable and validated to be useful. Also to make it job related, observations should be made under circumstances likely to be encountered. Another limitation of this method is that the cost of development and administration of tests are high.

8. **Ranking Methods:** A ranking method involving collective judgement is particularly useful for comparison purposes. Especially when employees reporting to different supervisors need to be compared, individual statements, ratings or appraisal forms are not helpful. The method needs to involve an overall subjective judgement to which a multitude of additional facts and impressions can somehow be added.

The two most effective methods in this respect are discussed below. When these two techniques are combined with multiple rankings, they are among the best available for generating valid order-of-merit rankings for salary administration purposes (i.e. when same employees are appraised independently by two or more appraisers and their rankings are averaged using either of this methods).

- **Alternation Ranking:** This method involves ranking of employees from best to worst on the basis of a particular quality or qualities. A list of all the employees to be appraised is prepared and the names of under-performing employees are crossed on that list. Then the employee who is highest and lowest on the quality being measured are indicated on a form. This step goes on alternating between highest and lowest, until all the employees to be appraised have been ranked. This method is most popular as it's relatively easy to differentiate between the worst and the best employees as compared to ranking them.
- **Paired-comparison Ranking:** This method is similar to alternation ranking but considered as more precise. However it is extremely time consuming and unmanageable if there are large number of employees.

9. **Essay Method:** Under this method, the appraiser is required to write a short essay on employee's strengths, weaknesses, potential and so on. The appraiser describes the employee based on a number of broad categories, for example: (i) employee's strengths and weaknesses, (ii) his effectiveness, (iii) the jobs ably performed by him, (iv) his training and development needs and (v) overall impression about the employee. This method is most commonly used in combination with others to fill the information gaps about the employees that often occur in the checklist method. It can particularly be helpful for selection purpose to take essay appraisals from former employers, teachers or colleagues.

10. **Cost Accounting Method/Human Asset Accounting Method:** This method evaluates an employee based on the costs incurred on him and the monetary returns he derives to the organisation. Thus employees' performance is appraised on the basis of the cost and benefit relationship.

II. **Future Oriented Appraisal**
1. **Management by Objectives (MBO):** This is a management system and philosophy where the supervisor and subordinate mutually identify their common performance objectives and define each employee's responsibilities, This agreement is used as a guideline for operating the team and appraising the contribution of each of its members. This method encourages employees' participation and helps in avoiding the feeling that they are being judged by unfairly high standards.

Objectives:
- To emphasise on goals rather than method.
- To offer responsibility and accountability.
- To change behaviour and attitude towards getting the job done.
- To provide opportunities for participation in the goal-setting process.

Advantages:
- **Concentrates on Actual Outcomes:** Employees are judged on real outcomes and not on their potential for success or on someone's subjective opinion of their abilities.
- **Direct Results can be Observed Easily:** This technique recognises the fact that it is difficult to divide and analyse all the complex and varied elements that go to make up employee performance efficiently. If all the elements are put together, the performance can be directly observed and measured.

Limitations:
(i) **Idealistic Expectations:** This technique may result in impractical expectations about goals. Supervisors and subordinates need to do self-auditing and self-monitoring.

(ii) **Assessment Centre Method:** This technique was first adopted by the German Army to evaluate the soldiers' performance. It appraises employees in job-related stimulations using a number of assessors and a variety of procedures. This stimulation includes the qualities that managers feel are important for the job.

2. **Psychological Appraisals:** Here appraisals are conducted by psychologists. This method is typically used by large companies who can employ full-time industrial psychologists. They measure employee's future potential and not past performance based on his intellectual, emotional, motivational and other related characteristics. The process normally consists of in-depth interviews, psychological tests, discussions with supervisors and a review of other evaluations. This method is slow and costly and as the quality of the appraisal depends largely on the skills of the psychologists, some employees may object to this type of evaluation. However it is typically used to take placement and development decisions, to shape the career of bright and young employees, having considerable potential.

4.5.6 Factors Necessary for a Performance Appraisal Policy

A number of crucial decisions about employees are made on the basis of performance appraisal and hence it must be sound and effective. Given below are the essential characteristics of a sound performance appraisal policy:

1. **Reliability and Validity:** Appraisal system should provide consistent, reliable and valid outcomes which can protect the organisation even in legal matters. Consistency refers to agreement in ratings given by two equally qualified appraisers using the same appraisal technique. Validity refers to measuring what is supposed to be measured.
2. **Job Relative:** The appraisal technique should measure the performance and provide information on job related activities and areas.
3. **Standardised:** All the elements of the appraisal procedure should be uniform across the organisation, e.g. appraisal forms, procedures, administration techniques, ratings etc.
4. **Feasibility:** The techniques should be practically viable to implement and administer and constantly economical.
5. **According to Laws:** The appraisal procedure must be in accordance with the labour laws framed by the constitution.
6. **Trained Appraisers:** Appraisers should be trained to conduct appraisals efficiently.

4.5.7 Efficiencies of Performance Appraisal

The main advantages or importance of performance appraisal are:

1. **Performance Feedback**

Most employees are very interested in knowing how well they are doing at present and how they can do better in a future. They want this information to improve their performance in order to get promotions and merit pay. Proper performance feedback can improve the employee's future performance. It also gives him satisfaction and motivation.

2. **Employee Training and Development Decisions**

Performance Appraisal information is used to find out whether an employee requires additional training and development. Deficiencies in performance may be due to inadequate knowledge or skills. For example, a professor may improve his efficiency by attending workshops or seminars about his subject. Performance appraisal helps a manager to find out whether he needs additional training for improving his current job performance. Similarly, if the performance appraisal results show that he can perform well in a higher position, then he is given training for the higher level position.

3. **Validation of Selection Process**

Performance appraisal is a means of validating both internal (promotions and transfers) and external (hiring new employees from outside) sources. Organisations spend a lot of time and money for recruiting and selecting employees. Various tools used in the selection process are application blanks, interviews, psychological tests, etc. These tools are used to predict (guess) the candidate's performance on the job. A proper performance appraisal finds out the validity of the various selection tools and so the company can follow suitable steps for selecting employees in future.

4. Promotions

Performance appraisal is a way of finding out which employee should be given a promotion. Past appraisals, together with other background data, will enable management to select proper persons for promotion.

5. Transfers

Performance appraisal is also useful for taking transfer decisions. Transfers often involve changes in job responsibilities, and it is important to find out the employees who can take these responsibilities. Such identification of employees who can be transferred is possible through performance appraisal.

6. Layoff Decisions

Performance appraisal is a good way of taking layoff decisions. Employees may be asked to lay off, if the need arises. The weakest performers are the first to be laid off. If there is no performance appraisal, then there are chances that the best men in the department may be laid off.

7. Compensation Decisions

Performance appraisal can be used to compensate the employees by increasing their pay and other incentives. This is truer in the case of managerial jobs and also in the case of employees in non-unionised organisations. The better performances are rewarded with merit pay.

8. Human Resource Planning (HRP)

The appraisal process helps in human resource planning (HRP). Accurate and current appraisal data regarding certain employees helps the management in taking decisions for future employment. Without the knowledge of who is capable of being promoted, demoted, transferred, laid off or terminated, management cannot make employment plans for the future.

9. Career Development

Performance appraisal also enables managers to coach and counsel employees in their career development.

4.5.8 Limitations or Shortcomings of Performance Appraisal

In order to be successful, every organisation must have a concrete performance management system. Performance management simply means matching the knowledge, skills and attitudes of the employees as against the strategic objectives of the organisation. The system involves employee training and development, organisational restructuring etc. As such, a performance management system is complex because it involves employees, supervisors and strategic managerial personnel. Having so much importance in the organisation, the performance management system still faces certain limitations that are listed as below:

1. **Risk of Internal Competition:** In a performance management system, each employee competes with the other for status, money, power, designation etc. This could definitely lead to backstabbing and as a result overall failure of the performance effort. This could slowly lead to non-functioning of the department all together. Performance management system in no way promotes that there would be healthy competition in the organisation amongst the employees. And hence this is regarded as one of the limitations of performance management systems.

2. **Favoritism:** Managers usually depend and give instructions to one employee rather than giving it to 100 employees for the purpose of avoiding the mistakes and confusion. This might cause a feeling of discomfort and jealousy in the minds of the employee and they might feel that working hard is not valued because only Mr. XYZ is going to get good grades. Performance management system does not guarantee elimination of biases and favouritisms.

3. **Expensive and Time Consuming:** Performance management systems are costly and involve a lot of time for implementation. Performance management system requires employees with high competency and hence it involves extensive training and development activities. It can also happen that the project on which the employee was currently working gets lost as he is engaged in learning new skills. This leads to negative organisational performance.

4. **Manager's Dilemma:** If the manager is not able to perform his duty well or he himself is not very clear with performance management goals, the entire system of performance management might fail. It thus becomes very difficult to decide performance values, indicators and contributors for the measurement.

5. **Convoluted and Bureaucratic:** The company ends up hiring and training new personnel. Performance management creates a new organisational structure. Hence there is a possibility that there are more than one teams working in the same department. This leads to disturbed financial structure of the organisation.

4.5.9 Guidelines for Performance Appraisal and Good Practices

Performance management tells the employees what they have to do but having standards set for the performance management tells them how well they have to do a particular task. Implementing a performance management system must be considered as an equally important process in the organisation like any other business tool. Given below are the simple guidelines for performance management in the organisation.

1. **Checklist for performance management:**
   (a) Employee involvement in the decision making
   (b) Sharing the performance standard statement with the employees
   (c) Setting and communicating the expectations from the employees
   (d) Declaring the measurement tool of overall performance
   (e) Implementation of formal performance appraisal process annually or twice a year but having a feedback system run continuously in the organisation.
   (f) Including specific and to-the-point suggestions for improving the performance further.
   (g) Evaluation of the entire process as well as the outcome.

2. **Setting the objectives:** While implementing the performance management system in the organisation it must be carefully noted that the objectives behind having the system must be clearly communicated and understood by the employees. Any confusion or misunderstanding will not serve the purpose of enhancing the performance. The objectives stage also involves identification of high performance standard for the purpose of giving rewards.

3. **Performance planning:** Performance planning is the process of defining expectations, setting measures to analyze the performance level and identifying and allocating appropriate resources to execute the process of performance management. It should be carefully noted that the measures adopted by the organisation for the purpose of checking the performance must relate to the results or output given by the employees.

4. **Feedback:** Once the performance planning is done and it has started taking place in the organisation, timely and constructive feedback must be shared with the employees in order to improve their performance further. If there is no proper feedback, employees will not understand the exact level of performance expected by them and hence will never be eligible for rewards. Lack of rewards will demotivate the employee which will again impact the performance of the individual in the organisation. This vicious circle needs to be broken.

5. **Counselling:** This is the most important stage in the performance management system. Many a times it happens in the organisation that not every employee understands the standards and executes in exactly the same way as expected. There are some to whom the standard is not much clear and out of fear they never ask it to their subordinates or superiors. This leads to getting low grades during the performance management period. Such people need more attention and guidance on how to improve the performance level and be at par with the other employees in the team.

4.5.10 Good Practices of Performance Management in the Organisation

1. **Defining workers' participation in management:** Engaging the employees in the goal setting process helps the smooth conduct of performance management to a very large extent. Due to involvement in goal setting the employees understand clearly their role in the performance management process and also what level of performance is expected out of them. This leads to a win-win situation in the organisation and hence the very purpose of performance management is served.

2. **Performance review management:** Taking review, feedback and sharing it with the employees with the necessary changes in the system leads to a lot of trust and belongingness in the minds of the employees. They feel cared and become more conscious about their work and feel free to ask performance related queries. Performance review management helps to keep the overall environment of the organisation positive and healthy.

3. **Educating the leaders and managers:** To make any system successful in the organisation, it must be carefully noted that the leaders and managers of the organisation are properly aware of the duties they need to perform and the responsibilities they are supposed to shoulder. The managers and leaders must buy into the process in order to get more results out of the system.

4. **Give employees small and attainable goals:** To boost the morale and motivation of the employees, every organisation must encourage them by giving them small but attainable goals. This helps them to understand their mistakes and at the same time achievement of small goals gives them a lot of confidence to improve themselves further.

5. **Be thorough about measurement:** The success or failure of the performance management system depends largely upon how well the performance is measured

and how well the same is communicated to the employees. Performance measurement helps both, management as well as the employees to understand the gap between standard performance and actual performance and the same can be bridged at an early stage for further improvement in the overall organisational performance.

Points to Remember

- Rewards System is the programme initiated and implemented by the organisations to reward the performance and motivate employees on individual and/or group levels.
- Objectives of Reward System
    1. Improving Organisational Culture
    2. Increasing customer focus
    3. Attraction and retention
    4. Motivation of performance
- Components of Reward System
    1. Individual Growth
    2. Compelling future
    3. Positive Workplace
    4. Total Pay
- Elements of Employee Reward
    1. Base Pay
    2. Contingent Pay
    3. Allowances
    4. Total Earnings
    5. Employee Benefits
    6. Total Remuneration
    7. Non-Financial Rewards
- Pitfalls of Performance Management
    1. Achievement of Targets
    2. Lack of Integration
    3. Lack of Leadership Support
    4. Lack of Rewards

5. Lack of Monitoring
  6. Lack of Evaluation
  7. Design Challenges
  8. Implementation Failure
- Remedies for Pitfalls of Performance Management
  1. Design
  2. Integration
  3. Leadership
  4. Competence
  5. Implementation
  6. Motivation
  7. Reward System
  8. Communication
  9. Monitoring
  10. Evaluation
- Efficiencies of Performance Appraisal
  1. Performance Feedback
  2. Employee Training and Development Decisions
  3. Validation of Selection Process
  4. Promotions
  5. Transfers
  6. Layoff Decisions
  7. Compensation Decisions
  8. Human Resource Planning
  9. Career Development
- Limitations or Shortcomings of Performance Appraisal
  1. Risk of Internal Competition
  2. Favouritism
  3. Expensive and Time Consuming
  4. Manager's Dilemma
  5. Convoluted and Bureaucratic

Questions for Discussion

1. What is the meaning, components and objectives of a reward system?
2. Explain the linkage between performance and reward and compensation system.
3. Discuss the performance management pitfalls and remedies for the pitfalls.
4. What are the efficiencies and limitations of the performance appraisal system?
5. Explain the guidelines for performance appraisal.

Project Questions

1. Most organisations find that employees come out with several grievances, once the appraisal is over and results are known through reward system. Why does this happen? Can you suggest some methods of performance assessment to avoid such outcomes?
2. You have an employee under you who has scored low on performance appraisal in all the areas. How would you plan the feedback session with him?

Chapter 5...
Ethics in Performance Management

Contents ...
5.1 Introduction
5.2 Ethical Performance Management
    5.2.1 Objectives of Ethics in Performance Management
    5.2.2 Significance of Ethics in Performance Management
    5.2.3 Ethical Issues in Performance Management
    5.2.4 Ethical Dilemmas in Performance Management
    5.2.5 Ethical Strategies in Performance Management
5.3 Performance Management in Multinational Corporations
- Points to Remember
- Questions for Discussion
- Project Questions

Learning Objectives ...
- To have a basic understanding of ethical performance management
- To be able to explain the objectives and significance of ethics in performance management
- To learn the ethical issues and dilemmas in performance management
- To understand the ethical strategies in performance management
- To study performance management in Multinational Corporations

5.1 Introduction

Ethics in performance management are considered to be the cornerstone of the process. In the process of managing and improving performance true and concrete feedback plays vital role. Overall objective of the Performance Management System of achieving high performance and greater productivity can be achieved only when the processes and people involved in the process are ethical. Hence the culture of ethics needs to be inculcated in the culture of the organisation. Honest assessment of the performance and equally honest feedback will help achieve this objective of bringing ethics in the performance management.

To get the trust and confidence of the employees on any process or function in the organisation, it is very essential that it is ethical in nature. The process must also teach ethics to the employees as to while managing their performance and going to the next level performance wise, the employees must take sincere efforts and even if it takes more time it must be honest in nature. Ethical performance management not only promises growth and development of the employee but also of the organisation as a whole.

Ethics basically means giving ethical treatment to the employees, stakeholders, owners, customers, society etc. When the business operates in an ethical fashion, the employees, the society starts trusting them and that helps to create goodwill and reputation in the minds of the customers, employees and everyone associated with the organisation.

Hence ethical operation will always help the organisation sustain in the competition for a longer period of time and help create a competitive advantage for itself. Because the primary objective of any organisation is to create and make profits for itself, but when it operates in an ethical way it automatically fetches more business towards it. Ethics and ethical behavior are the essential parts of any business entity and that show healthy business practices. In addition to that, ethical practices also ensure long term sustainability and competitive ability for the business.

5.2 Ethical Performance Management

Appraisal and managing of performance are subjective processes and there are a lot of chances that the processes will go wrong. Having biases and prejudices in the mind of manager appraising a particular employee will definitely impact the performance grade and also feedback on the performance improvement and as the process is subjective, it leaves employees reviews open to possible ethical complications. If a manger takes personal feelings into account while assessing an employee's performance, it is firstly unfair for the employee and secondly it is very likely to disturb the grades he deserves to have.

Ethics in performance management plays a vital role in the overall development of the organisation as well as employees. By having ethics in performance management the organisation should ensure honest and sincere effort in sharing the performance feedback with the employees. Also the feedback should be free from biases and prejudices then only it can said to be ethical in nature.

The performance management activity itself is a feedback mechanism which focuses on improving the quality of work of employees by giving true and constructive feedback. If the feedback shared is not related or seems to be casual in nature, the employees might not take the performance management process very effectively and seriously. Once the employees loose interest in the process, it will be very difficult for the organisation to bring back the interest and develop their performance ahead. Also it must be remembered that the process of performance management and development must be as transparent as possible which would help to gain the trust and confidence of the employees.

Hence it is very essential to have the performance management process ethical in nature.

5.2.1 Objectives of Ethics in Performance Management

Managers themselves are always concerned about the ethical beliefs and behaviours of their employees. It is always advisable that the organisation has the culture of ethics. Every organisation is run on the basis of trust and the feeling of belongingness towards each other. This is possible only when both the management as well as employees believe in ethics and influences others to follow ethics. Given below are some of the objectives of bringing ethics into performance management

- **Reliability and Validity:** This is the most important objective of performance management system. Every employee is anxious to know how he/she has performed in the last quarter / year and what management is expected out of them. A concrete feedback and SMART (Specific, Measurable, Attainable, Realistic and Time bound) goals can be set in front of the employees only when they trust the feedback given by the management. And there comes reliability and validity part into picture. The data or the facts presented by the management must be trustworthy.

  Future requirements of training and development as well as transfer and promotion depend upon this data. If this step goes wrong, the manpower planning for next year is going to go for a toss. Similarly, it should be valid. Employees must be able to relate the feedback to the work that they are doing and must find ways by themselves for improving their current state of performance. To achieve this objective, brining ethics into the process of performance management is a must.

- **Job Relatedness:** This is the second most important objective behind having ethics in performance management system. The way the feedback needs to be reliable and valid at the same time, it must be related to the job that the employee is doing. For example, if a person is working as sales executive, his performance feedback must be related to selling techniques, maintaining database of clients etc. and not researching the area before selling.

  Giving unrelated feedback confuses the employee and he may not achieve the targets for next quarter or year. Job relatedness plays a vital role in improving the performance of the employees to a great extent. When the employees receive feedback about the work that they are doing and it is perfectly on time that clicks them. They will always remember the feedback that was given to them on time and which was related to the kind of work that they have undertaken.

- **Standardisation:** This is a third and by far the most important objective why ethics should be in performance management. Standardisation is the process of developing and implementing technical standards (Wikipedia). If a standard is set, it becomes easier for the management to measure the performance and it is also beneficial for the employees as they get to know what level of performance is expected out of them in order to get a pay hike or promotion. When standards are set, the process becomes even more transparent as both the parties to performance management get to know their roles and confusion has no role to play.

  Standards always act as a benchmark in any activity. When you have a benchmark set it becomes easier for the employees to know where exactly you need to reach and what skills and competencies are required by the employees in order to reach the standards. Hence standardising the process makes the system much more ethical than before.

- **Practical Viability:** This is the forth important objective regarding why ethics in performance management are required. The standards that are set must be practical and also the feedback shared by the management should be practical in nature. Practical means achievable and can be performed in reality. This is again a very critical issue in the performance management process. The standards that are set in front of the employees regarding performance management must be practical and realistic in nature. This means they must be achievable in practice. If the standards that are set are too theoretical and closely impossible to achieve, then employees will easily lose interest in between and might not enjoy the performance management activity with commitment and enthusiasm.

In fact, the performance improvement activity is a very interesting phenomenon and employees enjoy if the goals and objectives are made clear to them. Once they know the importance of improving the performance, they enjoy the process of self-discovery and take honest efforts to improve their performance at work. This makes the process convenient for the management as well as for the employees.

- **Legal Sanction:** It should have legal compliances with the legal provisions concerned of the country. Legal sanction is a very critical issue in this regards. When we talk about ethics, legality of the object and actions surely comes into picture. Whatever plan the organisation has in mind for the employees it must be ethical in nature and at the same time it must be legally acceptable. Otherwise the employees would be trapped in the legal formalities.

  Having illegal objective or illegal processes not only disturbs the employees' working but also reduces the commitment and goodwill of the organisation from the minds of internal as well as external customers. Hence, legal sanction for each and every activity carried out by the organisation must be obtained.

- **Due Process:** Formal procedures should be developed to enable employees to pursue their grievances and having them addressed objectively. As discussed in the earlier chapters, performance management is a process and not a onetime activity. There are certain steps that are needed to be followed in order to get desired level of output and performance.

  Once the process is set and is shared with the employees who are a part of performance management programme, half of the work is already done. When employees are fully aware of the process, they know it very well as to what level of performance leads to what. They can assess their own performance and seek assistance wherever needed. Having transparency in the process increases trust and belongingness towards the organisation and management.

5.2.2 Significance of Ethics in Performance Management

1. **Asset Protection:** When there is a strong culture of ethics in business, employees tend to be more careful and consider themselves accountable for all the actions they perform. Employees can respect the assets of the organisation only when

organisation show them respect and dignity. This needs to reflect in every step organisation takes and hence same is applicable while sharing the performance feedback with the employees.

The feedback even if it is not positive must be shared in such a way that it encourages the employee to perform better the next time i.e. it should not demotivate him/her. A demotivated employee is likely to be rough and casual while handling the assets of the business. e.g. If the performance feedback is not shared and discussed properly, the employee may might use the business line for making long distance personal calls for a longer time.

2. **Productivity and Teamwork:** Business ethics are most important when it comes to increasing the productivity and teamwork amongst the employees. Like it is mentioned in the earlier points that to increase the productivity, it is very important to improve the performance. For this timely feedback and post performance appraisal discussion must take place.

   Because an employee needs to know where he is going wrong exactly and what he needs to do in order to make his performance count. Similarly every employee must take the criticism positively and consider it as a chance to prove him/herself. If each employee performs at this the level of productivity team work will reach new heights. This is possible when the entire process of performance management is ethically driven.

3. **Public Image:** The one, who makes ethical choices, earns a lot of respect and establish a strong image in the public. This is possible by shouldering corporate social responsibility ethically. If the organisation where you are serving, has a respectable name in the society, you will definitely think a thousand times before committing any unethical act.

   Productivity can be increased only if the performance of the employees is in line with the expectations of the organisation. When all the employees in the organisation are performing well, automatically the public image of the organisation in the eyes of the society goes up.

4. **Decision Making:** Ethical manner of the organisation supports decisions based on ethics. The role of decision making in performance management comes at the time of giving performance grades to the employees and also on deciding the performance linked benefits to the employees. Ethical decision making enhances

accountability and transparency in the entire process and employees consider the process as trustworthy.

An ethical decision making process makes the overall process of performance management concrete as it is the last step in the performance management. (feedback)

5.2.3 Ethical Issues in Performance Management

Ethical issues increase in the area of performance management. Areas of ethical misconduct under performance management include performance linked cash and incentive plans, performance appraisal, job discrimination, restructuring and layoffs etc. Let us see each of them in detail:

1. **Performance Linked Cash and Incentive Plans:** This usually includes deciding the base salaries depending upon the grades a particular employee has received. The issue here is, the HR department is forced to design high-salary-incentive plan in order to retain the employee in the organisation. Hence, many a times the grades shared through the process of performance management may not be true.

   Ethical issue arises when the HR department is put to pressure to favour the executives' interests over those of other employees. Thus, the performance linked cash and incentive plans need to be closely monitored in order to avoid any kind of ethical issue.

2. **Performance Appraisal:** Performance appraisal in itself gives space to ethical issues. Appraisal of individual's performance is based on observation and judgment. Here there is a lot of scope to be biased and have prejudices in mind.

   Many managers rate a particular employee depending upon the unrelated factors. Ethics must be the foundation stone of performance evaluation. High ethical performance review must provide honest and true feedback to all the employees and mutually develop a strategy to bridge the gap between actual performance and standard performance

3. **Job Discrimination:** Job discrimination refers to making adverse decisions against employees based on their membership to a certain group. Bringing in job discrimination in the process of performance evaluation and management is not at all advisable. The employee must be evaluated and guided on the basis of the work that he has done in the past or he is doing currently.

Personal prejudices, sex, race, cast, creed must be kept away from this process. Involving them in the system of performance management can only give false results and as an outcome, the employee and/or the organisation will not able to grow further in the long run.

4. **Restructuring and Layoffs:** Restructuring and layoffs are ethically important. If they are conducted in a positive and transparent manner, it could really turn ethical. However, there are a lot of chances that there could be unethical practices followed in the organisation regarding laying off a particular employee. This must happen in a fair environment and the employee must be laid off with respect and dignity

5.2.4 Ethical Dilemmas in Performance Management

While planning for ethical performance management, the HR department is faced with a lot of ethical dilemmas. The ethical dilemmas arise from three sources: Face to Face ethics, Corporate Policy Ethics and Functional areas ethics. Let us look at them one by one.

1. **Face to Face Ethics:** Since performance management system is one of the functions of HR department, it involves a lot of human element in most of the transactions. Employees in each department in the organisation are connected to each other and transact with each other for some or the other work. And there is no such formal relationship that exists between the two parties.

   For example, The Quality Assurance Manager might overlook a minor defect in the goods supplied by the supplier and approve a lot of order from him only because of the relationship both of them enjoy. Similarly, it is very likely that the manager over rates the performance of a particular employee because of the similar relationship existing between the two. Thus, this ethical dilemma in performance management must be avoided.

2. **Corporate Policy Ethics:** Companies are frequently faced with ethical dilemmas that influence processes across all departments and divisions. Following contradictory situations are typical:

   (a) You are interviewing ex- product manager who just left a competitor's company. You are thinking of hiring him. He would be more than happy to tell you the competitor's plans for the coming years. What would you do?

   (b) You have just finished appraising your team's performance. One your team member has not performed up to the mark in the past quarter but you know that he is really a good employee and has a potential to do big wonders for the organisation where he serves. Through your performance assessment, he has received the lowest grade and you very well know that this is going to demoralise him even more. What would you do?

Many a times, it happens that you want to assess the performance of the employee by keeping in mind quantitative as well as qualitative aspects. But corporate policy ethics does not allow this all the time. And hence in situations like these, the managers are faced with corporate policy ethics dilemmas.

3. **Functional Area Ethics:** Functional areas of business confront ethical issues. To avoid functional area ethical dilemmas, organisations are required to adopt certain standards. Like for example, relating to preparation of financial statements, standards like Generally Accepted Accounting Standards (GAAPs) should be adopted, whose main purpose is to establish unform standards for reporting financial statements etc.
Similarly in case of managing performance of the employees and thereby of the entire organisation, standards like PCMM (People Capability Maturity Model) must be adopted that helps the organisation to measure its performance as well as its employees' performance.

5.2.5 Ethical Strategies in Performance Management

To improve the overall system of performance management and make it ethically stronger, certain ethical strategies must be adopted while assessing the performance. The list of these strategies is given as follows -

1. **Quality:** While assessing the performance of the employee or while planning for managing and improving his/her performance, quality aspect should be of primary focus. By quality we should know that the degree to which the employee has carried out the particular activity, the time period taken by him/her to finish the task and whether he has fulfilled the task's intended purpose. If a particular employee satisfies these conditions of quality, his performance should be assessed positively accordingly.

Quality is a very important aspect of performance management programme. If the employee is not doing quality work it is not of any use. Hence performance management activity strives to improve the performance of the employees by improving the quality aspect simultaneously. Once the quality is managed in performance management it helps to reduce the costs, supports differentiation, and respond to various strategies that are planned by the organisation for the employees.

2. **Quantity:** This standard of performance management is purely quantitative and solely depends upon the amount of goods produced. This must be expressed in monetary terms. This represents the number of items produced in a particular time frame and the number of activities completed in a given time frame. Hence the manager while assessing the performance of the employee must look at the quality aspect of the goods produced, at the same time the number of such quality units produced in a given period of time. Then only the assessment will have a holistic overview.

   The way quality aspect in performance management is important, similarly quantitative aspect is also equally important. The standards that are to be set by the management must define units. Once the employees know the amount of units they must achieve in order to improve the current performance level, it becomes easier to measure the performance of the employees. And further changes in the performance can be made easily.

3. **Timeliness:** Keeping a time frame or finishing the work in time must be given more priority than the one taking a lot of time to finish the tasks. Because producing 1000 units is not an achievement but producing 1000 units in 1 hour is really commendable. Rewarding an employee finishing his/ her work in time with less errors and wastages must get higher grades than others. If every manager follows this principle, the process of performance management will be more ethical.

   Timeliness regarding work and also about the feedback is equally important. While rewarding or appraising the performance of the employee it must ascertained whether he has completed the work in a given time frame or not. And the rewards for the performance even if it is good quality wise must be given when the employee has finished it within the timeframe. By linking rewards to timely submission makes the employees aware of the importance of finishing the tasks on time. Meeting the deadlines and completing the tasks on time also gives a feeling of satisfaction to the employees and their commitment and belongingness towards the organisations also improves.

4. **Cost Effectiveness:** Cost effectiveness is also called as "ROI" i.e. return on investment or alternatively it is called as optimum utilisation of human and organisational resources. Cost effectiveness technique must be adopted by each and every employee in order to maximise the output and reducing the level of errors in each of

the units. The same principle must be used while appraising the performance of the employee. The one who is the most cost conscious or cost effective in his/her approach, must be rewarded with higher grades and linked benefits.

Cost effective or cost conscious is the appropriate word for the employee who performs in such a way that it leads to fewer mistakes and good quality at work. The employee who saves the costs of the organisation is considered to be the best performer in the organisation. Hence quality and cost consciousness must go hand in hand in performance management programme in the organisation.

5. **Need for Supervision:** The need for supervision must be the least in the organisation. The employees in the organisation must be empowered and given enough autonomy to take decisions, plan the activity and work in such a way that it helps the employee to achieve personal as well as organisational objective. The employees who need little or no supervision at all constitute a team called as High Performance Team, which are the need of the hour. The employees who are motivated and extremely committed to their role and organisation require less supervision and they prefer working on their own. Their understanding of the performance criteria and working on accomplishment of the goals on their own. This should be taken care of while assessing the performance of the employees.

6. **Interpersonal Impact:** The degree to which a performer promotes feeling of self-esteem, goodwill, and co-operation among co-workers and subordinates. This is again a qualitative aspect of performance assessment but this is considered in the 360 degree appraisal of an employee. His/her relations with others and his/her thoughts about oneself must be given a lot of value as this feeling about oneself generates motivation or demotivation in the minds of the employee.

5.3 Performance Management in Multinational Corporations

Performance Management in multinational companies is the most challenging task of International Human Resource Management Department. Its main task is to assess the performance of the employees as well as of other various activities in the organisation.

Performance management may be understood as a process that enables a multinational corporation to assess and facilitate continuous improvement programme for individuals, processes, functions, departments etc. The performance management process in case of multinational companies is slightly different which is shown in the diagram below:

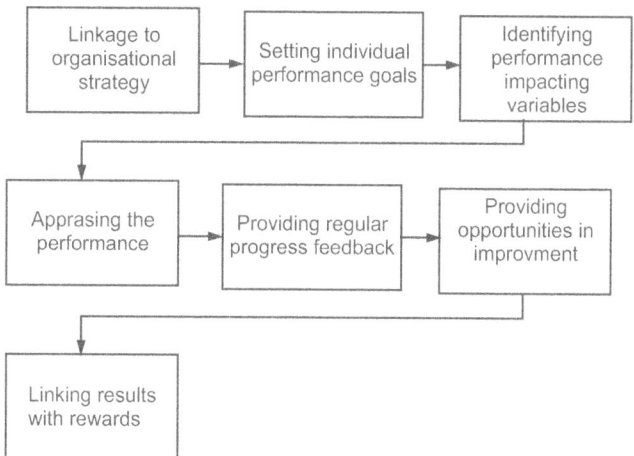

Fig. 5.1: Performance Management Process in Multinational Companies

1. **Linking with organisational strategy:** In MNCs, performance management becomes an integral part of each and every function. If the organisation doesn't perform up to the mark it may have to take its steps back from the competition. Hence, if the performance management activities are linked with organisational strategies, they will not only enhance the performance of the employees but also establish strategies for reward linking and identify employee needs for further development. All these collectively offer strong inputs for strategy formulation and implementation in the organisation.

   Any initiative that is started in the organisation must necessarily get linked with the organisational vision, mission and objectives. If there is no match between the organisational strategy and performance management strategy, the entire efforts of performance management and improvement will go waste. Hence while planning for performance goals and objectives, it must be critically monitored that they are in line with the strategic objectives of the organisation and organisation is going to be equally benefitted with the performance management initiatives adopted by the management.

2. **Setting individual Performance goals:** As the organisation progresses, it might happen that the goals are set only for the growth and expansion of the business and in this the employee's growth and development take a back seat. However this is not at all an advisable practice in the MNCs. When individuals develop, the entire organisation develops. It should also be remembered that the goals set for the employees must be SMART goals i.e. Specific, Measurable, Achievable, Rational, Time Bound.

Setting up individual performance goals has become the need of the hour. In order to achieve holistic results, it is very essential to have individual employee developed. The meaning of performance management itself is understanding the nature and strengths and weaknesses of the individual employees and accordingly design performance management process for them. By designing the process in this way, the employee feels cared and motivated to take up the challenge of self improvement and at the same time his commitment level towards the organisation also improves. Thus, setting individual performance goals is essential.

3. **Identifying variables impacting the performance:** It always happens that what you write on paper and the reality has a wide gap. This gap needs to bridged in order to make the performance management process effective. There are usually two main factors that impact the performance of an employee viz., intrinsic factors such as challenging job, career prospects etc. and extrinsic factors viz., working conditions, company policies etc. If these variable are identified at an early stage they can be removed easily and further performance can be improved for the betterment of the individual as well as organisation. While planning for performance management in the organisation it must be identified that what are the factors that cause disturbance in the performance management process.

When these factors are identified at an early stage, the performance can be improved at a faster rate and the chances of mistakes and errors reduce to a greater extent later on. The identification of the factors can take place only when there is a strong feedback mechanism present in the organisation. Due to timely and regular feedback it becomes easier for the employees to correct their performance and management can understand if something is going wrong during the execution of performance plans.

4. **Appraising the performance:** Performance appraisal or assessment of the performance is a routine task that involves checking the performance of the employees against the standard set and making certain key decisions on the basis of that. In MNCs, the culture is highly process oriented unlike Indian corporations. Hence those employees would be values whose performance meets the standards. Thus, appraising performance of the employee and sharing true feedback becomes the most important part of the performance management process.

Performance appraisal is no doubt one of the most important parts of performance management plan. During the performance improvement initiative, if the employees do not receive assessment of their performance, they will not understand whether their performance is going on a right track or not and as a result they might feel lost in between. Performance appraisal reviews the performance of each employee against the standard set for him/her and provides input for improving the performance further.

5. **Providing regular feedback on progress towards goals:** Feedback refers to the information provided to the employee about work behaviour and outcomes. And as mentioned in the earlier point, sharing timely and true feedback helps the employee to take corrective action for the performance pitfalls. Early detection of problems saves a lot of time in the future.

   Thus, providing regular feedback on the performance as well as how far the employee has contributed towards achievement of the organisational goals needs to be communicated to each of the individual. Like appraisal, it is very essential to have a strong feedback mechanism present in the organisation. Appraisal cannot happen every week or every month and hence strong feedback mechanism always helps in improving the performance of the employees. This also helps in early detection of errors and there is also a scope for improvement in the performance plan if the need be.

6. **Providing opportunities for improvement:** Performance feedback also helps in highlighting the need for training and development. As discussed earlier, early detection of the problem, helps to take immediate corrective action to avoid future problems. This helps to provide opportunities to MNCs to improve, socialise and adjust to new environments ably. Once the employees receive regular and timely feedback they become more focused towards their work and seek for improvements. This is a good sign for the organisation.

   The performance management process must always strive for awakening the inner drive of the employees towards the performance improvement. When they themselves will feel from within the need for performance improvement, things would change.

7. **Linking Results with Rewards:** The final activity in managing the performance system for MNCs is linking the output with rewards. By rewards we mean

consideration or something in return. Rewards must necessarily follow performance. If rewards are exciting, the employee works doubly hard to achieve them. So if the organisation wishes that its employees show belongingness and perform up to the mark, enough rewards should be given to the employees.

This is indeed the most important part in performance management. When the performance of the employees is rewarded they feel more positive with their work and their concentration at work increases. The reward could be monetary or non-monetary but it must be noted that it should be exciting and encouraging enough. The reward acts as an impetus to the employees to perform even better the next time to get even a better reward. The reward based performance management plans always prove to be satisfactory and enhance the commitment level of the employees at work.

Points to Remember

- Ethics in performance management plays a vital role in the overall development of the organisation as well as employees. By having ethics in performance management the organisation should ensure honest and sincere effort in sharing the performance feedback with the employees.
- Objectives of Ethics in Performance Management
    1. Reliability and Validity
    2. Job Relatedness
    3. Standardisation
    4. Practical Viability
    5. Legal Sanction
    6. Due Process
- Significance of Ethics in Performance Management
    1. Asset Protection
    2. Productivity and Teamwork
    3. Public Image
    4. Decision Making
- Ethical Issues in Performance Management
    1. Performance Linked Cash and Incentive Plans

2. Performance Appraisal
   3. Job Discrimination
   4. Restructuring and Layoffs
- Ethical Dilemmas in Performance Management
   1. Face to Face Ethics
   2. Corporate Policy Ethics
   3. Functional Area Ethics
- Ethical Strategies in Performance Management
   1. Quality
   2. Quantity
   3. Timeliness
   4. Cost Effectiveness
   5. Need for Supervision
   6. Interpersonal Impact

Questions for Discussion

1. What do you understand by the term ethical performance management? Explain the objectives and significance of ethics in performance management.
2. Discuss the ethical issues and dilemmas in performance management.
3. Explain the ethical strategies in performance management.
4. How performance management in Multinational Corporations is different from domestic corporations?

Project Questions

1. As a manager, what steps would you take if your performance management system has a desperate and adverse impact? Discuss.
2. Do you think the performance management system will convert the employees into better employees?

Case Studies

Case Study 1: Performance Management at Network Solutions, Inc. 1

Network Solutions, Inc., is a worldwide leader in hardware, software and services essential to computer networking. Until recently, Network Solutions, Inc., had over 50 different systems to measure performance within the company, many employees did not receive a review, fewer than 5 per cent of all employees received the lowest category of rating, and there was not a recognition programme in place to reward high achievers. Overall, there was recognition that performance problems were not being addressed, and tough pressure from competitors increased the costs of not managing human performance effectively. In addition, quality initiatives (Six Sigma) were driving change in several areas of the business, and Network Solutions decided that these initiatives should also apply to 'people quality'.

Finally, Network Solutions wanted to improve its ability to meet its organisational goals, and one way of doing this would be to ensure they were linked to each employee's goals. Given the situation described above, in 2001 Network Solutions' CEO announced he wanted to implement a forced distribution performance management system in which a set percentage of employees are classified in each of several categories (e.g., rating of 1 to the top 20 per cent performers, rating of 2 to the middle 70 per cent performers, and rating of 3 to the bottom 10 per cent performers). A global cross-divisional HR team was put in place to design and implement the new system. The first task for the design team was to build a business case of the new system by showing that, if organisational strategy was carried down to team contributions and team contributions were translated into individual goals, then business goals would be met. Initially the programme was rolled out as a 'year round people management system that raises the bar on performance management at Network Solutions by aligning individual performance objectives with organisational goals by focusing on development of all employees'.

The desired outcomes of the new system included raising the performance level of all employees, identifying and retaining top talent, and identifying low performers and improving their performance.

Network Solutions also wanted the performance expectations for all employees to be clear.

Before rolling out the programme, the design team received the support of senior leadership. They did this by communicating that the performance management system is the future of Network Solutions, and by encouraging all senior leaders to ensure that their direct reports understood the process and also bought into it. In addition, they encouraged senior leaders actually to use the system with all of their direct reports, and to demand and utilise output from the new system. Next, the design team encouraged the senior leaders to stop the development and use of any other performance management systems, and pushed for standardisation of performance management across all divisions. Finally, they had senior leaders call attention to the new programme by involving employees in training about talent management and assessing any needs in their divisions that the new system would not address.

The Network Solutions global performance management cycle consists of the following process:

1. Goal cascading and team building
2. Performance planning
3. Development planning
4. Ongoing discussions and updates between managers and employees
5. Annual performance summary

There are training resources available on Network Solutions' intranet for managers and individual contributors, including access to all necessary forms. In addition to the training available on the intranet,

1–2 hour conference calls took place before each phase of the programme was rolled out.

Part of the training associated with the performance management system revolves around the idea that the development planning phase of the system is the joint year-round responsibility of managers and employees. Managers are responsible for scheduling meetings, guiding employees on preparing for meetings, and finalising all development plans. Individual contributors are responsible for documenting the developmental plans. Both managers and employees are responsible for preparing for the meeting, filling out the development planning preparation forms, and attending the meeting.

With forced distribution systems, a set number of employees must fall into set rating classifications.

As noted above, in the Network Solutions system employees are given a rating of a 1 (given to the top 20 per cent of employees in the performance distribution), 2 (given to the middle 70 per cent of employees in the performance distribution), or 3 (given to the bottom 10 per cent of employees in the performance distribution). Individual ratings are determined by the execution of annual objectives and job requirements as well as a comparison rating of others at a similar level at Network Solutions.

Employees receiving a 3, the lowest rating, have a specified time period to improve their performance. If their performance does improve then they are released from the plan, but they are not eligible for stock options or salary increases. If performance does not improve, they can take a severance package and leave the company, or they can start on a performance improvement plan that has more rigorous expectations and timelines than the original action plan. If performance does not improve after the second period, their employment is terminated without a severance package. Individuals with a rating of 2 receive average to high salary increases, stock options and bonuses. Individuals receiving the highest rating, 1, receive the highest salary increases, stock options and bonuses. These individuals are also treated as 'high potential' employees and given extra development opportunities by their managers. The company also makes significant efforts to retain all individuals receiving this rating.

Going forward, there is a plan to continue reinforcing the needed cultural change to support forced distribution ratings. HR centres of expertise continue to educate employees on the system to ensure that they understand that Network Solutions still rewards good performance; they are just measuring it differently. There is also a plan to monitor for and correct any unproductive practices and implement correcting policies and practices. To do this they plan on continued checks with all stakeholders to ensure that the performance management system is serving its intended purpose.

Consider Network Solutions' performance management system in light of what we discussed as an ideal system. Then, answer the following questions:

1. Overall, what is the overlap between Network Solutions' system and an ideal system?
2. What are the features of the system implemented at Network Solutions that correspond to what the module described as ideal characteristics? Which of the ideal characteristics are missing? For which of the ideal characteristics do we need additional information to evaluate whether they are part of the system at Network Solutions?

3. Based on the description of the system at Network Solutions, what do you anticipate will be some advantages and positive outcomes resulting from the implementation of the system?
4. Based on the description of the system at Network Solutions, what do you anticipate will be some disadvantages and negative outcomes resulting from the implementation of the system?

Case Study 2: Employee Performance Appraisal System for Jelly Belly

Candy making is a fun business, and so it's no surprise that it's fun to work at the Jelly Belly Candy Company of Fairfield, California. But at this family-owned company, there's no fooling around when it comes to promoting employee performance and job satisfaction. So when Jelly Belly decided to overhaul and automate its antiquated employee performance and talent management process, it was looking for a serious solution to help give its employees across the United States fair, accurate performance appraisals.

Herman Goelitz Candy was founded in 1869 by Albert and Gustav Goelitz, whose great-grandsons own and run Jelly Belly today. The Jelly Belly Candy Company makes Jelly Belly brand jelly beans in over 50 flavours, as well as candy corn and other treats. Introduced in 1976 and named by former U.S. president Ronald Reagan as his favourite candy, the company's jelly beans are exported worldwide.

Like almost every smart company, Jelly Belly recognizes that employees are more likely to stay with their employer when they feel connected and recognised for their efforts. Programmes for managing and evaluating employee performance are critical to aligning corporate and employee values and priorities.

Challenge

Jelly Belly's search for a new employee performance and talent management system began several years ago, when two branches of the family business were reunited into a single company. One branch was using an outdated performance management software programme. The other was doing its employee performance appraisals manually, using paper forms.

Having a variety of jelly bean flavours is great — a variety of employee appraisal processes in a single company is not. The task of updating and consolidating the performance management process fell to Margie Poulos, HR Manager of Jelly Belly's Midwest operations. She and a small team of Jelly Belly HR staff were charged with finding a single automated system that could be used for all of Jelly Belly's 600 employees in three locations.

The driving factor behind Jelly Belly's performance management automation was the belief that thorough, accurate reviews help employees to better understand what's expected of them, so that they can set clear, measurable objectives. That translates into higher employee satisfaction, said Jeff Brown, Jelly Belly's Director of Human Resources. "When employees feel they have gotten a thorough and accurate review, it boosts their morale," Brown said. It also leads to improved talent management and makes it easier to retain valuable employees, which management experts know is a key factor in corporate growth and market leadership.

Case Study 3: DMADV Case Study: Performance Management System Redesign

To facilitate the development of its employees and better respond to the changing business environment, one department of a large financial-services company decided to revamp its existing performance management system through a Six Sigma project. A pre-project analysis revealed that a complete redesign of the system was required. As incremental improvement in the existing system was not possible, the project team followed the Design for Six Sigma (DFSS) DMADV (Define, Measure, Analyze, Design, Verify) roadmap, incorporating best practices from Six Sigma, project management and information technology (IT) service management. This case study covers a few major aspects of the project, which could readily be applied in similar situations across various industries and business environments.

Define Phase

In the Define phase, the team created a goal statement: To implement a comprehensive, well-aligned and consistent performance management system for Department A.

The team looked at the existing performance management system. It had the following prominent attributes:
- The system supported all product lines of Department A, covering more than 200 employees.
- The implementation and usage of the system was limited to individual departments.

- The company had functional silos, and employee goals were determined within the department.
- Unit managers (there were multiple units within each line of business) were responsible for setting performance targets for their units.
- Individual performance was compared against the set target.

Measure Phase

As part of the Measure phase of the project, the team analysed the existing performance management system. Then by interviewing key stakeholders, team members identified what the company wanted from such a system.

In particular, the improvement team focused on the identification of:

- Most useful features of the current system
- Not-so-useful features
- Missing features (i.e., needed improvements)

When interviewing managers, team members asked the following questions:

- How can this system help you in coaching, performance appraisal and decision making?
- What information do you want to receive in order to develop and maintain employee and service performance?

The team further had to consider these factors for the performance management system:

- **Frequency:** How often should metrics be updated?
- **Availability:** At what time should the performance management system should be available?
- **Security:** Who should be able to see what information?
- **Continuity:** Is it a business-critical application? What needs to happen during/after a disaster?
- **Capacity:** How many users need to be supported? How much data needs to be stored?

Analyse Phase

Based on the information gathered during the Measure phase, the team identified the vital problems of the existing system and derived key requirements for the new system as an output of the Analyse phase (table below).

Deriving the Key Requirements of a New Performance Management System

Problem with Existing System	Key Requirement for New System
Managers were able to influence the targets heavily and were setting up lenient targets. Thus, a lot of employees were rated high performers while the business was not benefiting equally.	• Head of department to set product-line targets. These targets should be used to compare roll-up level metric values to determine each unit's performance. • Current achieved performance levels at unit and department level should be used to derive the future performance targets.
Performance metrics and ratings across product lines were not standardised, thus making it very difficult to translate and roll up metrics from individual employee to department level.	Standardise performance management process, metrics and ratings to enable quick understanding of process, roll-up of metrics and comparison of employees across product lines.
Performance metrics were available only at the end of the month, making it difficult for managers and individual associates to take corrective action proactively.	System should be refreshed daily to provide up-to-date information.
Productivity was weighted much higher than quality. The focus on productivity came at the expense of quality.	Equal importance to be given to productivity and quality. Department head should also have a mechanism to change relative importance according to business need.
Individuals within each product line were compared against each other, even if performing different tasks. This comparison was not standardised, making entire system biased toward some types of tasks.	Set up peer groups to enable fair comparison. Together with standardised performance metrics and ratings, this should enable comparison across the board.
Individual employees did not have access to their own performance metrics, thus hindering self-directed performance improvements.	Each employee should have access to their own performance metrics and should have a way to compare it against the baseline and against the peer group.
Month-over-month metric trends were not available. Creating such a trend report required a lot of manual effort.	Month-over-month metrics values and trends should be automatically generated. Also, provide a facility to select the reporting period.

Design Phase

With its functional silos, the business environment was not conducive to a solution that incorporated a balanced scorecard approach. The functional silos made it difficult to cascade organisational-level targets to departmental-level targets and further to individual-level targets. Due to these reasons, a balanced scorecard approach was eliminated from the scope of the project.

Because a key requirement of the new performance management system was to move from using a fixed-target system to a dynamic-target system, two alternatives for measuring baseline performance were thoroughly explored: 1) the best known performer, also referred to as *k-performer*, and 2) the average performer. Ultimately the department decided to go with average performance as the baseline.

Before the decision was made to move from a fixed-target-based system to one based on a dynamic target, there was much deliberation on that question. Some of the prominent points that came out of those discussions would be of interest to all practitioners:

- A fixed-target system provides visible targets to employees. Typically, it does not require complex calculations and makes it easy for individual employees to determine their own rating solely based on their own performance. On the other hand, the dynamic-target determination system (either best performer as baseline, or average performer as baseline) makes it difficult to determine the target and leaves employees with some guess work until the final performance targets are derived and announced.

- A fixed-target system is susceptible to violations. Targets could be set so that they are either too strict or too lenient. A dynamic-target determination system fills this gap. It is also self-corrective in nature, and adapts itself according to business and employee performance. For example, in a fixed-target system if there is not enough work to achieve productivity targets, employees would not have enough opportunity to meet the targets and would be rated "below target." The dynamic target determination system would accommodate such fluctuations and is thus a more robust system.

- Setting the k-performer as a baseline would make the entire population's performance ranking highly vulnerable to the performance of one individual. This is similar to the impact that an outlier can have on a set of data. Setting the average performance as a baseline reduces this vulnerability, making the system more robust.

Equipped with input from stakeholders and the derived requirements for a new performance management system, the team moved forward with a solution following these five steps:

1. Identification of alternatives
2. Comparison of alternatives
3. Selection of the most feasible alternative
4. Creation of an implementation plan
5. Implementation of the solution

Those steps were considered from both a functional and an IT perspective.

Verify Phase

As part of process control, a technique for automated data validation and verification was employed. This technique helps indicate any out-of-order data point to line managers and the department director. These out-of-order data points and any other significant events are recorded in an event log. An incident log has been established to capture various incidents that take place with respect to the performance management system. The event log and the incident log play a pivotal role in the identification of improvement opportunities.

About 12 months after implementation, the system has been performing to expectations. An evaluation to either maintain the status quo or to improve the system further would be made as part of the strategic planning session for the following year.

Case Study 4: Bringing performance management to life

Steps creates a half day programme designed for HSBC managers in India, to help them develop their performance management skills and conduct more effective meetings with their reports.

Objective

Somshukla Ghosh, Senior Vice President of Performance & Rewards at HSBC in Mumbai commissioned Steps to create a half day programme designed for managers, to help them develop their people skills in order to conduct excellent performance management meetings with their reports.

The managers had previously received theoretical training around the HSBC Performance Management process, but it was felt that the managers needed to further develop their one-to-one people skills and effective management behaviours. HSBC were looking for a practical, interactive, engaging and memorable method of training. Tanuj Kapilashrami, HR Director of HSBC Mumbai had seen Steps in action at a diversity seminar hosted by the bank in March 2010 and recommended our work.

Approach

Steps delivered five half day programmes during one week in June 2010 at the HSBC Mumbai Training Centre. A total of ninety-two managers of various grades attended the programme. The three hour course was delivered by Robbie Swales, a director of Steps and Mohan Madgulkar, Steps' Senior Associate from Pune.

The use of drama for learning and development is a relatively new concept in India. However, having over fifteen years of experience in this field, Steps combined knowledge and experience to tailor the intervention, ensuring it was reflective of the the banks culture and Indian context. Mohan interviewed a dozen stakeholders at HSBC to discover the culture of the bank and understand the HSBC Performance Management Process. He also spoke at length to Natasha Pinto, the Associate Vice President of Performance Management, to establish the key objectives of the training initiative. Steps then wrote the programme and delivered a pilot to the HR Heads of Business, whose feedback was incorporated into the final programme to be delivered to the managers.

The three hour programme incorporated two interactive scenarios. These both focussed on the appraisal process, with an actor-facilitator playing the manager asking the delegates for advice, and then weaving that advice back into the scenario. This engaging method enabled the delegates to focus on the types of behaviours that would help managers to run effective appraisals. The delegates were also split into small groups, and asked to share their thoughts on what constitutes good performance management. The delegates also made commitments to actions during the session, to sustain the learning and the momentum for positive change.

Outcomes

The training was very well received, with attendees reporting an increase in confidence of 19%. 93% of delegates rated the course as Good or Excellent – and one participant commented. "The most valuable aspect was the way the session was delivered. Highly interactive and participative. Excellent!!" This sentiment was echoed by Natasha Pinto, who remarked; "Steps' session was fantastic for engaging our senior teams and improving working practices at HSBC. The intervention was high impact and has delivered measurable results.'

Case Study 5: Case of Ethics in Performance Appraisal

Frank became chief financial officer and a member of the Executive Committee of a medium-sized and moderately successful family-owned contracting business six months ago. The first non-family member to hold such a position and to be included in the Executive Committee, he took the job despite a lunch-time remark by the company's CEO that some members of the family were concerned about Frank's "fit with the company culture." But the CEO (who is married to the daughter of the founder of the company) said he was willing to "take a chance" on Frank.

Soon after Frank started, the company decided for the first time to "right-size" (a euphemism for downsize) to respond to rapid changes in its business. Frank, who had been through this before when he was a senior manager in his previous company, agreed this was good for the long-term health of the 20-year-old company. He decided not to worry that family members seemed more concerned about their own short-term financial interests.

Besides, the CEO was relying on Frank to help him determine how to downsize in an ethical manner; the CEO said he trusted Frank more on this than he did the head of his personnel department, who had "been around a little too long."

On Frank's recommendation, the company decided to make its lay-off decisions based on the annual performance appraisal scores of the employees. Each department manager would submit a list of employees ranked by the average score of their last three appraisals.

If the employee had been with the company less than three years, if the score for two employees was identical, or if there was some extraordinary circumstance, the manager would note it and make a decision about where to rank the person. At some point, Frank and the Executive Committee would draw a line, and those below the line would be laid off.

As Frank was reviewing the evaluations, he was puzzled to find three departments in which the employee at the bottom of the list had "N/A" where the evaluation score should have been written. When he asked the managers to explain, they told him these employees had been with the company almost since the beginning. When performance appraisals had been instituted six years earlier, the CEO agreed to the longtime employees' request that they keep receiving informal evaluations "as they always had."

The managers told Frank they'd questioned this decision, and the CEO had told them it wasn't their problem.

When Frank raised this issue with the CEO, he responded, "Oh, I know. I haven't really evaluated them in a long time, but it's time for them to retire anyway. They just aren't performing the way they used to. The company's been very good to them. They've got plenty of retirement stored away, not to mention the severance you've convinced me to offer. They're making pretty good money, so cutting them should let us lower the line a little and save jobs for some of the younger people--you know, young kids with families just starting out. And don't worry about a lawsuit. No way they'd do that."

"Do they know they're not performing well?" Frank asked.

"I don't know," the CEO responded. "They should. Everybody else in the company does."

As they walked to the door, the CEO put his arm around Frank's shoulder. "By the way," he said, "you should know that you've won over the Executive Committee. They think you are a terrific fit with this company. I'm glad you talked with me today about these three employees. You got it right: This is a company that cares for its employees--as long as it can and as long as they're producing. Always has, always will."

Frank left the CEO's office with the vague feeling that he had some moral choices to make.

Does he have an ethical dilemma? What's the right thing to do? If he disagrees with the CEO, how does he protect his own career and the interests of his own family? What do you think?

Case Study 6: Dealing with Poor Performance

Carol is a claims administrator with Rest Assured plc, a life assurance company. In her mid 60s, she is one of the company's longest-serving employees and has an unblemished disciplinary record. David, the claims team manager, who joined the company recently, arranges a meeting with the HR manager, Elaine, to discuss a problem he is having with Carol. Some of Carol's colleagues have complained to him that she is not pulling her weight and is dealing with her claims allocation very slowly. They have to cover for her to prevent a backlog of claims building up.

David explains to Elaine that he has been told that Carol's poor performance has been a problem for some time but the previous claims team manager did nothing about it. There is no documentation showing that the problem was being addressed. The previous manager allowed Carol to coast along, so much so that it appears to Derek that she has become somewhat "set in her ways". Because of the effect that Carol's underperformance is having on the rest of the team, David wants to take decisive action now.

Elaine needs to outline to David the steps that he should take to address Carol's underperformance. He should take action promptly before Carol's performance issues escalate further, and follow a performance management procedure. He must also take care to comply with the requirements of the Acas code of practice on disciplinary and grievance procedures (PDF format, 1MB) (on the Acas website), which covers poor performance However, before he takes formal action against Carol, David must investigate whether or not she is underperforming and, if she is, why. He will need to meet Carol to discuss the possible cause of her below-standard job performance. He should make it clear to her that this meeting is investigatory and is not, at this stage, part of the formal disciplinary process.

Prior to the meeting, David should collect relevant and objective evidence, for example customer complaints and other evidence to demonstrate that Carol has not been dealing with claims in a timely manner. If they had been available, he would also have needed to obtain copies of Carol's appraisals and details of discussions that her previous manager had with her concerning her performance.

Assuming that the evidence indicates that Carol has been underperforming, based on the evidence that he collects and his subsequent meeting with Carol, David should try to establish whether Carol's underperformance is capability or conduct related, and whether or not there are mitigating reasons for it.

Poor performance that is capability related may be attributable to inadequate or insufficient training, poor communication, the employee's lack of understanding of his or her goals and objectives, lack of feedback, poor quality supervision and/or support, excessive workloads, unrealistic targets and deadlines, poor working relationships and personal problems. Alternatively, poor performance may be the result of genuine inability or lack of commitment. If Carol's poor performance is conduct related, Rest Assured should follow its disciplinary procedure rather than a performance management process.

If David identifies that Carol's poor performance is capability related, he should agree specific action points and targets with her, together with a realistic timescale in which she should achieve them. He should also arrange training or other remedial steps if these are appropriate and schedule a follow-up meeting to review Carol's performance.

It is essential that David keep a record of the meeting (including the agreed targets for improvement) and of the arrangements for the follow-up meeting. He should continue to monitor Carol's on-going performance. If Carol's performance does not improve after Rest Assured has followed their performance management procedure, he may be left with no alternative but to take this to a formal review panel.

To avoid Carol being able successfully to claim any kind of unlawful discrimination against Rest Assured, for example because of her age, David should deal with her performance in the same way as he would for other employees in the team. Prior to this, subject to the (now repealed) statutory retirement procedure, employers could compulsorily retire employees when they reached retirement age. As a result, many employers overlooked performance issues in older members of staff who were approaching retirement age because they would be leaving anyway. David cannot use the fact that Carol may have attained what was previously the company's retirement age as a reason to end her employment. Nor can he assume that she will want to retire at this point. If he treats Carol less favourably than other employees because she is close to, or has reached, a particular age, this might amount to unlawful age discrimination. Conversely, if he treats her more leniently than other members of the team for the same reason, Rest Assured could be vulnerable to claims of age discrimination by them.

David gathers his evidence and meets with Carol to discuss his concerns. At first Carol is defensive and claims that her performance is no worse than that of the other members of the claims team. She does not believe that there have been customer complaints about her so she cannot see what the problem is. However, when David shows her evidence that her closure rate of claims files has consistently been the lowest in the team and that some customers have complained about the slow handling of their claims, she breaks down in tears and confesses to David that she has been struggling to cope with the volume of work since a new computer system for handing claims records was installed over a year ago. Although she received training when the new system was introduced, she is not as computer literate as some of the other members of the team and has struggled with it.

Having established that Carol's performance issue is capability and not conduct related and that her underperformance appears to be due to a training need, David decides to take an informal approach. He tells her that she needs to improve her performance or she may be moved to the next stage of the performance management process, which could ultimately lead to formal warnings.

David arranges for Carol to receive one-to-one refresher training on the new claims records system. Once the training is complete, David agrees with Carol that, over a period of three months, she must ensure that her claim closure rates are at, or above, the claims team's average. He also agrees with her that he will sit down with her at the end of each month during this period to discuss how she is progressing towards meeting the target and any concerns that she may have.

At the end of the three-month period, Carol's performance shows a consistent improvement and the informal approach has serves its purpose without need to move to more formal measures. He continues to monitor her performance by way of regular meetings and Rest Assured's appraisal process.

David's experience with Carol demonstrates the benefits for employers of having robust and fully documented processes and of dealing with performance issues as and when they arise. Employers that have failed to address poor performance at the outset may have to tolerate a longer period for improvement than they otherwise would, because the employee will have become used to performing at the lower level. It is important to have some documented evidence of a performance issue before starting formal action and by carrying out an investigation into the poor performance, the employer should be able to identify whether it is due to capability or conduct, and follow the correct procedure as a result.

Multiple Choice Questions

1. Performance Management is a primary HRM Process that links employees and organisations and provides input for other processes through these means:
   (a) Identification, measurement, management
   (b) Assessment, direction, development
   (c) Recruitment, selection, on boarding
   (d) Skills, efforts, responsibility

2. Measuring performance is based on a measurement approach that can be broken down to type of judgment and measurement focus. Which of the following is the way to appraise performance based on measurement?
   (a) Trait　　　　　　　　　　(b) Behaviour
   (c) Outcome　　　　　　　　(d) Relative

3. A number of potential problem areas may affect the quality of performance measurement results in performance management. Select the correct alternative.
   (a) Rater errors and bias　　　(b) Influence of liking
   (c) Organisational politics　　(d) All of the above

4. The systematic management of the individual's performance on the job is called _____.
   (a) Performance Management　(b) Job evaluation
   (c) Job description　　　　　(d) Job analysis

5. Which of the following does not relate to performance management?
   (a) Objectives of performance management
   (b) Establishment of job expectations
   (c) Designing appraisal programmes
   (d) Organisational climate indices

6. Which of the following relates to rater?
   (a) Immediate supervisors　　(b) Subordinates
   (c) Peers　　　　　　　　　　(d) All of the above

7. Behaviourally Anchored Rating Scales is also called as _____.
   (a) Behavioural expectation scales　(b) BARS
   (c) Field review method　　　　　　(d) Both 'a' and 'b'

8. Confidential records are maintained mostly in _____
   - (a) Government Departments
   - (b) Private departments
   - (c) Educational institutions
   - (d) Industry and companies

9. Management By Objectives (MBO) concept was conceived by _____
   - (a) L.J. Lindley
   - (b) B.O. Wheeler
   - (c) Y.K. Bhushan
   - (d) Peter F. Drucker

10. A formalised effort that recognises employees as valuable organisational resources and focuses on developing them to their fullest practical performance potential is _____
    - (a) Career Development
    - (b) Training Development
    - (c) Potential Development
    - (d) Executive Development

11. The process of evaluating an employee's current and/or past performance relative to his or her performance standards is called ____.
    - (a) recruitment
    - (b) employee selection
    - (c) performance appraisal
    - (d) organizational development
    - (e) training

12. When goal setting, performance appraisal, and development are consolidated into a single, common system designed to ensure that employee performance supports a company's strategy, it is called ____.
    - (a) strategic organizational development
    - (b) performance management
    - (c) performance appraisal
    - (d) human resource management
    - (e) strategic management

13. Performance management combines performance appraisal with ____ to ensure that employee performance is supportive of corporate goals.
    - (a) goal setting
    - (b) training
    - (c) incentive systems
    - (d) all of the above
    - (e) none of the above

14. Managers following a performance management approach to appraisals will usually meet with employees on a ____ basis.
    (a) weekly
    (b) monthly
    (c) bi-annual
    (d) yearly
    (e) bi-monthly

15. Managers following a traditional performance appraisal system will typically meet with employees on a ____ basis.
    (a) daily
    (b) weekly
    (c) monthly
    (d) bi-monthly
    (e) yearly

16. The component of an effective performance management process that explains each employee's role in terms of his or her day-to-day work is called ____.
    (a) role clarification
    (b) goal alignment
    (c) developmental goal setting
    (d) direction sharing
    (e) coaching and support

17. Which of the following is not one of the guidelines for effective goal setting?
    (a) assign specific goals
    (b) assign measurable goals
    (c) assign challenging but doable goals
    (d) assign consequences for performance
    (e) encourage participation

18. The S in the acronym for SMART goals stands for ____.
    (a) specific
    (b) straightforward
    (c) strategic
    (d) source
    (e) support

19. The M in the acronym for SMART goals stands for ____.
    (a) moderate
    (b) measurable
    (c) meaningful
    (d) mid-range
    (e) merit

20. The A in the acronym for SMART goals stands for ____.
    (a) actionable
    (b) appropriate
    (c) attainable
    (d) attitude
    (e) asset

21. Participatively set goals result in higher performance than assigned goals when ____.
    (a) participatively set goals are more difficult
    (b) assigned goals are more difficult
    (c) the rewards are also higher
    (d) participatively set goals are used consistently
    (e) the goals are doable

22. Who is the primary person responsible for doing the actual appraising of an employee's performance?
    (a) the employee's direct supervisor
    (b) the company appraiser
    (c) the human resource manager
    (d) the EEO contact person
    (e) none of the above

23. Which of the following is not a role played by the HR department regarding performance appraisals?
    (a) Training of supervisors
    (b) Monitoring the appraisal system
    (c) Appraising of employees
    (d) Ensuring compliance with EEO laws
    (e) Advising regarding appraisal tools and procedures

24. When designing an actual appraisal method, the two basic considerations are ____.
    (a) who should measure and when to measure
    (b) when to measure and what to measure
    (c) what to measure and who should measure
    (d) what to measure and how to measure
    (e) when to measure and how to measure

25. The most popular technique for appraising performance is the ____ method.
    (a) alternation ranking
    (b) rating scale
    (c) Likert
    (d) MBO
    (e) constant sum rating scale

26. Which performance appraisal technique lists traits and a range of performance?
    (a) alternation ranking
    (b) rating scale
    (c) Likert
    (d) MBO
    (e) constant sum rating scale

27. What do performance appraisals measure?
    (a) generic dimensions of performance
    (b) performance of actual duties
    (c) employee competency
    (d) achievement of objectives
    (e) all of the above

28. If a performance appraisal focuses on an employee's ability to "identify and analyse problems" or to "maintain harmonious and effective working relationships," then the performance appraisal is focused on measuring ____.
    (a) generic dimensions of performance
    (b) performance of actual duties
    (c) employee competency
    (d) achievement of objectives
    (e) all of the above

29. If a performance appraisal focuses on an employee's quality and quantity of wok, then the performance appraisal is focused on measuring ____.
    (a) generic dimensions of performance
    (b) performance of actual duties
    (c) employee competency
    (d) achievement of objectives
    (e) all of the above

30. Suppose you have five employees to rate. You make a chart of all possible pairs of employees for each trait being evaluated. Then, you indicate the better employee of the pair for each pair. Finally, you add up the number of positives for each employee. In this case, you have used the ____ method of performance appraisal.
    (a) graphic ranking scale
    (b) constant sum ranking scale
    (c) alternation ranking
    (d) paired comparison
    (e) forced distribution

31. Forced distribution refers to an appraisal method, which ____.
    (a) is based on progress made toward the accomplishment of measurable goals
    (b) combines the benefits of narratives, critical incidents, and quantified scales by assigning scale points with specific examples of good or poor performance
    (c) requires that the supervisor keep a log of positive and negative examples of a subordinate's work-related behaviour
    (d) requires a supervisor to evaluate performance by assigning predetermined percentages of those being rated into performance categories
    (e) involves listing all the subordinates to be rated, crossing out the names of any not known well enough to rank, indicating the employee who is the highest on each characteristic being measured and who is the lowest, and then alternating between the next highest and lowest until all employees have been ranked

32. When a supervisor evaluates performance by assigning predetermined percentages of ratees into performance categories, he or she has used the ____ method of performance appraisal.
    (a) graphic ranking scale
    (b) constant sum ranking scale
    (c) alternation ranking
    (d) paired comparison
    (e) forced distribution

33. John, the supervisor of the manufacturing department, is in the process of evaluating his staff's performance. He has determined that 15% of the group will be identified as high performers, 20% as above average performers, 30% as average performers, 20% as below average performers, and 15% as poor performers. John is using a ____ method.
    (a) graphic rating scale
    (b) constant sum ranking scale
    (c) forced distribution
    (d) alternation ranking
    (e) paired comparison

34. Which of the following measurement methods rates employee performance relative to other employees?
    (a) graphic rating scale
    (b) forced distribution
    (c) likert scale
    (d) constant sums rating
    (e) critical incident method

35. With the _____ method, the supervisor keeps a log of positive and negative examples of a subordinate's work-related behaviour.

    (a) alternation ranking
    (b) constant sums rating
    (c) forced distribution
    (d) narrative forms
    (e) critical incident

36. The critical incident technique refers to an appraisal method, which _____.

    (a) is based on progress made toward the accomplishment of measurable goals
    (b) combines the benefits of narratives, critical incidents, and quantified scales by assigning scale points with specific examples of good or poor performance
    (c) requires that the supervisor keep a log of positive and negative examples of a subordinate's work-related behaviour
    (d) requires a supervisor to evaluate performance by assigning predetermined percentages of those being rated into performance categories
    (e) involves listing all the subordinates to be rated, crossing out the names of any not known well enough to rank, indicating the employee who is the highest on each characteristic being measured and who is the lowest, and then alternating between the next highest and lowest until all employees have been ranked

37. All of the following are advantages of using the critical incident method for appraising performance except that _____.

    (a) it provides examples of good performance
    (b) it does not include a numerical rating
    (c) it provides examples of poor performance
    (d) it reflects performance from throughout the appraisal period
    (e) incidents can be tied to performance goals

38. Which appraisal method combines the benefits of narratives, critical incidents, and quantified scales by assigning scale points with specific examples of good or poor performance?

    (a) behaviourally anchored rating scale
    (b) graphic rating scale
    (c) constant sums rating scale
    (d) alternation ranking
    (e) none of the above

Performance Management   Multiple Choice Questions

39. Behaviorally anchored rating scale (BARS) refers to an appraisal method, which ____.
    (a) is based on progress made toward the accomplishment of measurable goals
    (b) combines the benefits of narratives, critical incidents, and quantified scales by assigning scale points with specific examples of good or poor performance
    (c) requires that the supervisor keep a log of positive and negative examples of a subordinate's work-related behaviour
    (d) requires a supervisor to evaluate performance by assigning predetermined percentages of those being rated into performance categories
    (e) involves listing all the subordinates to be rated, crossing out the names of any not known well enough to rank, indicating the employee who is the highest on each characteristic being measured and who is the lowest, and then alternating between the next highest and lowest until all employees have been ranked

40. The first step in developing a behaviourally anchored rating scale is to ____.
    (a) develop performance dimensions   (b) generate critical incidents
    (c) reallocate incidents   (d) scale incidents
    (e) develop a final instrument

41. All of the following are advantages of behaviourally anchored rating scales (BARS) except that they ____.
    (a) are more accurate
    (b) provide clearer standards
    (c) are time consuming
    (d) are reliable
    (e) help explain performance appraisal ratings to appraisees

42. Management by objectives (MBO) refers to an appraisal method, which ____.
    (a) is based on progress made toward the accomplishment of measurable goals
    (b) combines the benefits of narratives, critical incidents, and quantified scales by assigning scale points with specific examples of good or poor performance
    (c) requires that the supervisor keep a log of positive and negative examples of a subordinate's work-related behaviour
    (d) requires a supervisor to evaluate performance by assigning predetermined percentages of those being rated into performance categories

(e) involves listing all the subordinates to be rated, crossing out the names of any not known well enough to rank, indicating the employee who is the highest on each characteristic being measured and who is the lowest, and then alternating between the next highest and lowest until all employees have been ranked

43. Which of the following is a problem with using MBO?
   (a) a tendency to set unclear objectives
   (b) a tendency to set unmeasurable objectives
   (c) it is time consuming
   (d) tug of war between subordinate and manager regarding goals
   (e) all of the above

44. Graphic rating scales are subject to all of the following problems except ____.
   (a) unclear standards   (b) halo effects
   (c) complexity   (d) central tendency
   (d) leniency

45. When different supervisors define levels of performance (good, fair, poor) differently, unfair appraisals could result due to a problem with ____.
   (a) unclear standards   (b) halo effects
   (c) complexity   (d) central tendency
   (e) leniency

46. ____ is defined as the influence of a rater's general impression on ratings of specific ratee qualities.
   (a) Impression management   (b) Halo effect
   (c) Central tendency   (d) Stereotyping
   (e) Bias

47. Jason is generally considered unfriendly at work. His supervisor rates him low on the trait "gets along well with others" but also rates him lower on other traits unrelated to socialization at work. Jason's performance appraisal may be unfair due to ____.
   (a) impression management   (b) bias
   (c) stereotyping   (d) halo effects
   (e) strictness

48. Some supervisors, when filling in rating scales, tend to avoid the highs and lows on the scale and rate most people in the middle. This _____ means that all employees may be rated average.
    (a) halo effect
    (b) stereotyping
    (c) central tendency
    (d) strictness
    (e) leniency

49. The best way of reducing the problem of central tendency in performance appraisals is to _____.
    (a) rank employees
    (b) be aware of the problem
    (c) train supervisors to avoid it
    (d) impose a distribution for performance
    (e) consider the purpose of the appraisal

50. The _____ problem occurs when supervisors tend to rate all their subordinates consistently high.
    (a) central tendency
    (b) leniency
    (c) strictness
    (d) bias
    (e) halo effect

51. The _____ problem occurs when supervisors tend to rate all their subordinates consistently low.
    (a) central tendency
    (b) leniency
    (c) strictness
    (d) bias
    (e) halo effect

52. The best way of reducing the problems of leniency or strictness in performance appraisals is to _____.
    (a) rank employees
    (b) be aware of the problem
    (c) train supervisors to avoid it
    (d) impose a distribution for performance
    (e) consider the purpose of the appraisal

53. When an employee's personal characteristics such as age, race, and gender influence a supervisor's evaluation of his or her performance, the problem of _____ has occurred.
    (a) bias
    (b) stereotyping
    (c) central tendency
    (d) halo affect
    (e) strictness

54. Which of the following could result in a legally questionable appraisal process?
    (a) conduct a job analysis to establish criteria and standards for successful performance
    (b) base appraisals on subjective supervisory observations
    (c) administer and score appraisals in a standardised fashion
    (d) use clearly defined job performance dimensions
    (e) avoid abstract trait names when using graphic rating scales

55. Who is in the best position to observe and evaluate an employee's performance for the purposes of a performance appraisal?
    (a) peers
    (b) customers
    (c) rating committees
    (d) top management
    (e) immediate supervisor

56. Performance appraisals may be conducted by ____.
    (a) the immediate supervisor
    (b) peers
    (c) rating committees
    (d) subordinates
    (e) all of the above

57. Peer appraisals have been shown to result in a(n) ____.
    (a) reduction of social loafing in the team
    (b) reduction of group cohesion
    (c) decrease in satisfaction with the group
    (d) lower task motivation
    (e) tendency to inaccurately predict who would be promoted

58. What usually occurs when employees rate themselves in a performance appraisal?
    (a) interrater reliability is higher
    (b) appraisals are subject to halo effects
    (c) logrolling could occur
    (d) ratings are higher than when rated by supervisors or peers
    (e) ratings are about the same as when determined by peers

59. Firms that use ____ let subordinates anonymously rate their supervisor's performance.
    (a) downward feedback
    (b) upward feedback
    (c) MBO
    (d) narratives
    (e) critical incidents

60. What process allows top management to diagnose the management styles of supervisors, identify potential "people" problems, and take corrective action with individual supervisors as necessary?
    (a) strategic performance appraisal   (b) organisational development
    (c) upward feedback   (d) MBO
    (e) critical incidents

61. What is another term for 360-degree feedback?
    (a) feedback loop   (b) multi-source assessment
    (c) upward feedback   (d) circle feedback
    (e) wheel feedback

62. You are conducting an appraisal interview with an employee who is satisfactory, but not promotable. Which incentive listed below would likely be the least effective for maintaining satisfactory performance in this situation?
    (a) time off   (b) small bonus
    (c) compliments   (d) additional professional development
    (e) additional authority

63. Which is the easiest type of appraisal interview to conduct?
    (a) satisfactory-not promotable   (b) satisfactory-promotable
    (c) unsatisfactory-correctable   (d) unsatisfactory-uncorrectable
    (e) final warning

64. When conducting an appraisal interview, supervisors should do all of the following except ?
    (a) talk in terms of objective work data
    (b) compare the person's performance to a standard
    (c) encourage the employee to talk
    (d) give specific examples of poor performance
    (e) compare the person's performance to that of other employees

65. Which of the following responses is not typical during a negative appraisal interview?
    (a) denial   (b) anger
    (c) relief   (d) aggression
    (e) retreat

66. When a supervisor must criticise a subordinate in an appraisal interview, it is best to ____.
    (a) hold the meeting with other people who can diffuse the negative situation
    (b) provide examples of critical incidents
    (c) acknowledge the supervisor's personal biases in the situation
    (d) provide feedback once per year
    (e) surprise the employee so they cannot develop excuses for poor performance

67. Subordinates may feel dissatisfied with their appraisal interview when they ____.
    (a) feel threatened during the interview
    (b) have an opportunity to express their ideas
    (c) have an opportunity to influence the course of the interview
    (d) have a constructive interviewer conduct the interview
    (e) are shown specific examples of their poor performance

68. When an employee's performance is so poor that a written warning is required, the warning should ____.
    (a) identify the standards by which the employee is judged
    (b) provide examples of employees who met the standards
    (c) provide examples of times when the employee did meet the standards
    (d) be sent to the employee in question, to the manager's superior, and to the EEO office
    (e) all of the above

69. Performance Appraisal is a part of _____
    (a) People management   (b) Performance management
    (c) Process management   (d) Policy management

70. _____ is defined as a multi step process of aligning employees work behaviours with the strategy and goals of the organization
    (a) Performance appraisal   (b) Performance management
    (c) Performance planning   (d) Performance analysis

71. _____ refers to a system of moral principles.
    (a) Values   (b) Beliefs
    (c) Thoughts   (d) Ethics

72. Performance management essentially consists of _____
    (a) Performance Planning
    (b) Performance analysis
    (c) Performance development and audit
    (d) All of the above

73. _____ is the process of assessing the performance and progress of an employment on a given job and his potential for future development.
    (a) Counselling
    (b) Potential appraisal
    (c) Performance appraisal
    (d) Coaching

74. The aim of performance management is to _____
    (a) Ensure employee's performance is supporting the company's strategic aims
    (b) Consolidate goal setting
    (c) Ensure employee has the tools needed to perform the job
    (d) Evaluate employee's performance against standards

75. A common way of determining a fair reward for a fair performance is based on ____
    (a) Friendship
    (b) Contribution
    (c) Merit
    (d) Heritage

Answer Key

1. (c)	2. (c)	3. (d)	4. (a)	5. (d)	6. (d)	7. (d)	8. (a)	9. (d)	10. (a)
11. (c)	12. (b)	13. (d)	14. (a)	15. (e)	16. (a)	17. (d)	18. (a)	19. (b)	20. (c)
21. (a)	22. (a)	23. (c)	24. (d)	25. (b)	26. (b)	27. (e)	28. (c)	29. (a)	30. (d)
31. (d)	32. (e)	33. (c)	34. (b)	35. (e)	36. (c)	37. (b)	38. (a)	39. (b)	40. (b)
41. (c)	42. (a)	43. (e)	44. (c)	45. (a)	46. (b)	47. (d)	48. (c)	49. (a)	50. (b)
51. (c)	52. (d)	53. (a)	54. (b)	55. (e)	56. (e)	57. (a)	58. (d)	59. (b)	60. (c)
61. (b)	62. (d)	63. (b)	64. (e)	65. (c)	66. (b)	67. (a)	68. (a)	69. (b)	70. (b)
71. (d)	72. (d)	73. (c)	74. (a)	75. (c)					

www.ingramcontent.com/pod-product-compliance
Lightning Source LLC
Chambersburg PA
CBHW080925180426
43192CB00040B/2709